H.M.S. OCEAN

1945 - 1957

Peacetime Warrior

By
Joyce Knowlson

*With very best wishes Mitie,
Biggles, Bigglesdor, and
Bigglesdor's Mum*

Dedication

For John - without whom this book would never have been written.

TABLE OF CONTENTS

Foreword

Among the ships in which I served, HMS OCEAN was very special. She was hard-worked - operations never far from and often beyond the limits, every ounce of effort demanded of man and machine. She broke records; the country has not had better value for money.

A wealth of informative detail on the ship, much of which has been provided by members of the HMS OCEAN ASSOCIATION, has been collated by the Secretary Mrs Joyce Knowlson, whose hard work demands our thanks. That a group of ex-OCEANs should have formed such a world-wide and active Association is a reflection upon the bonds which grew and still exist between those who served in that busy ship.

I am delighted to have been invited to write this foreword.

Rear Admiral Euan Maclean. CB.

HMS Ocean 1761 - 1783

The first OCEAN was a ' wooden wall' , a 90 gun second rate, 176ft x 49ft and built in Chatham Dock-yard in 1761.   From 1772 - 1776 she was the Flagship in Plymouth and in 1778 she joined the Channel Fleet which was then commanded by Admiral Keppel.   The American War of Independence had begun in 1775 and in February 1778 France made a Treaty of Commerce and Alliance with the Americans fol-lowed in the same year by a Declaration of War against England.

H.M.S OCEAN, as part of the fleet, participated in three encounters during this period.   The first took place 108 miles N.W by N. of Ushant when Admiral Augustus Keppel, who had put to sea on 9th July 1778 with a fleet of ships, including OCEAN commanded by Captain John Laforey, met with the French fleet, under the command of Admiral d'Orvilliers who had earlier left Brest. The battle on 27th July 1778 was inconclusive and there was no loss of ships on either side but the English casualties were higher than those of the French. It was the only significant encounter between the British and French fleets in home waters in the American War.

The second action occurred on 12th December 1781.   A force of twelve of the line, commanded by Rear Admiral Richard Kempenfelt, intercepted a convoy of merchant ships bound for the West Indies carrying supplies and reinforcements.   An escort of nineteen French Naval vessels, under the command of Rear Admiral de Guichon accompanied them.   The action was carried out 160 miles SW of Ushant and as the convoy was separated from the Naval force they scattered but 15 prizes were captured by the English without loss. This action is commemorated in the first Battle Honour awarded to OCEAN - Ushant 1781.

On 20th October 1782 the English fleet was in action once more.   Admiral Viscount Howe with a force of thirty three ships, including OCEAN commanded by Captain George Ourry fought the combined force of French and Spanish ships in a successful action 45 miles off Cape Spartel.

On 10th January 1783 OCEAN was paid off and later was later broken up at Plymouth in 1791.

Copyright Greenwich Maritime Museum

HMS Ocean 1795 - 1852

The second H.M.S OCEAN, a second rate of 98 guns, 197ft x 52 ft and 4047BM, was built in Woolwich Dockyard. She was launched on 24th October 1795 and commissioned on 3rd December 1795. From 1806 - 1809 she was the Flagship of Vice Admiral Lord Cuthbert Collingwood, Commander in Chief Mediterranean, and spent the first 18 months of service off the coast of Spain in the area of Cadiz. This was where many of the ships that had escaped capture at Trafalgar were laying low. Later the operations were switched Sicily and the area around Syracuse.

Between 1812 - 1814 OCEAN was employed as a private ship on blockade duty, still in the Mediterranean. In January 1817 she was reclassified as a 110 gun first rate operating on the Lisbon and Mediterranean stations until 1830 when she returned to Plymouth and was paid off. In 1831 OCEAN was brought back into commission and became harbour duty Flagship at Sheerness until 1835 before again laying out of commission until 1838. In that year she was recommissioned as guardship and depot ship, then from 1848 as Flagship, Nore, where she remained until 1851. In 1852 she became a coal hulk at Sheerness until finally being broken up at Chatham in 1875.

Copyright Greenwich Maritime Museum

HMS Ocean 1862 - 1872

The third OCEAN was laid down in 1860. She was intended to be a wooden wall ship of 91 guns but in 1861 the order was changed to an iron clad of 50 guns, 273 x 58ft, 6800BM and was fitted with a Maudsly Horizontal Reciprocating NHP 1000 engine plus eight rectangular 20lb pressure coal-fired boilers driving a four blade 21 inch propeller. Her sail area with double top sail totalled 25, 000 ft. She carried 500 tons of coal giving a steaming radius of 2000 miles at 5 knots

One of the CALEDONIA class, all three of which including PRINCE CONSORT were laid down in 1860, OCEAN was launched on 19th March 1862 and emerged finally with 24 x 7 inch muzzle loaded rifled guns and with a complement of 605 officers and men. Her armour consisted of lower deck and side belt 41 x 31 inch thick cladding of 935 tons.

The ship was assigned to the Far East, and enroute she set the record for the longest day's run by any British Ironclad under sail of 243 miles. OCEAN served on the China Station from 1867 as the Flagship of Commander in Chief, Vice Admiral Keppel and his successor Vice Admiral Kellet. After an active life of only six years she returned to Plymouth to pay off in 1872 and was then sold to Messrs Castle to be broken up in 1881.

Copyright Greenwich Maritime Museum

HMS Ocean 1898 - 1915

The fourth OCEAN was a first class battleship laid down at Devonport in 1897 and launched on 5th July 1898. One of the Canopus class, her sister ships were GOLIATH, ALBION, GLORY, VENGEANCE and CANOPUS itself. OCEAN was 400 ft x 74 ft, with a displacement of 12, 950 tons, and twin screws. Her armament comprised 4 x 12 inch, 12 x 12 pounder guns and 4 torpedoes. With a speed of 18 knot and a complement of 682 officers and men, the class was built to keep ahead of the Japanese fleet by strengthening the British China fleet. This class was the first to be fitted out with Krupp steel armour, which was about 50% stronger than Harvey steel and three times stronger than iron armour. They were also the first battleships to be fitted with water tube boilers which were small, lighter and more efficient than the previously used locomotive boilers .

OCEAN suffered several setbacks during build and gained the reputation of being an unlucky ship. Ninety feet of the ship fell like a pack of cards when the ribs collapsed. The building programme suffered a strike by engineering workers, and at the launch on 5th July 1898 the ship at first refused to move and there was an hours delay before Princess Louise could complete the launching ceremony. The ship gained a reputation as the ship ' that did not want to go to sea' . On 20th February 1900 the ship was commissioned and was transferred to the Mediterranean and then on to the China Station (one of the first British battleships able to take passage through the Suez canal) where she served from 1901 - 1905 during which time she was damaged by a typhoon and had several refits.

She returned from the Far East to be paid off and transferred to Chatham reserve, returning to active service with the Channel fleet in 1906. In 1908 she returned to the Mediterranean. On 4th July 1909 she joined the Home Fleet, remaining there until 1914 when she joined the 8th Battleship Squadron and sailed to Queenstown. At this time she was commanded by Captain Hayes Sadler and was employed protecting Persian Gulf convoys. On 25th January 1915, when Turkey was preparing to attack the Suez Canal, the ship was sent to cover the El Shatt operation. She took part in the capture of Qurra and Basra (Mesopotamia) in 1914 and two battle honours were awarded - Mesopotamia 1914 and Suez Canal 1915.

On 28th February 1915 OCEAN left Port Said for Tenedos for operations in the Dardanelles in the company of ALBION, IRRESISTIBLE, MAJESTIC, TRIUMPH and VENGEANCE. On 18th March 1915 IRRESISTIBLE was hit by fire from Turkish batteries on shore, while trying to force the narrows, OCEAN began to withdraw but was struck by a mine and then hit by a shell which caused flooding in the tiller flat and starboard steering compartments leaving the ship with irreparable damage. The ship was abandoned, with all hands safe, at 1930 and the finally came to rest in the depths of Marlo Bay at 2230 that same day. A battle honour was awarded, Dardanelles 1915.

H.M.S Ocean 1945

The Last Swordfish, the First Vampire

Not the largest of aircraft carriers, nor one of the best known, nevertheless the fifth H.M.S OCEAN had enough ' incidents' in her twelve years of life to make an interesting story.

The ship was laid down in 1942 at Alexander Stephens yard, Linthouse, Govan. She was a handsome ship of just over 13, 000 tons - 17, 720 tons full load. The launch ceremony was conducted at 1600 on Saturday July 8th 1944. It was preceded by a private lunch at the Central Hotel Glasgow with senior officials, after which Admiral Sir Algernon Willis, the Second Sea Lord, and his wife proceeded to Linthouse to tour the yard accompanied by Vice Admiral Sir James Troup, Flag Officer Glasgow. The ceremony was performed by Lady Olive Willis and was followed by a tea for fifty invited guests at which Lady Willis was presented with a diamond brooch by the shipbuilding company. An interesting note is that this brooch was purchased second hand from a London jewellers - a sign of the austerity of World War Two. At the end of 1945, before she sailed for the Mediterranean, Lady Willis made a further visit to OCEAN to present a cup, as a trophy, for the Ship's Company.

During the actual ceremony one of the attendant tugs ' Flying Spray', sustained an accident when a wire became lodged in her propeller and a diver had to be engaged to clear it. Clyde Shipping Company, the owners of the vessel, held the Stephens yard liable for the damage and claimed for consequent loss and damage.

The design of the ship was slightly modified during build to enable her to operate night fighter aircraft and she was fully equipped with the latest in Radar and aircraft direction devices. This was to later to prove significant.

OCEAN was commissioned on June 30th 1945 and on July 5th was towed down to the floating dock off Helensburgh until July 18th. Caspar John became the first Captain. A complex character - on one hand an eccentric bohemian, on the other a firm, fair and down to earth disciplinarian; famous for his bushy eyebrows and steely gaze. He was held in great respect by his ship's company and declared that his aim was "to make from a metal shell a liveable, happy community with a sense of purpose". The big problem at that time was that the war was over and with many experienced crew thinking of demobilisation he needed a hard core of men to give spine to the ship's company. His main priority was to maintain sustainable morale and welfare.

By early August the ship had completed full power trials and a week of flying trials. The first deck landing and take off was made by Lieutenant W. N. Preston flying a Barracuda MD761 on August 7th. On August 10th Lieutenant Commander E. M. Brown landed a Sea Hornet PX212, followed on the same day by Commander D. Robertson piloting a Sea Fury SR661. Later in the same month OCEAN left the Clyde for Liverpool Here Radar was fitted and a hole was made in the flight deck and hangar to enable Cammell Lairds to insert a new engine turbine replacement.

October saw the last official flight from a carrier deck by a Fairey Swordfish in which Vice Admiral Sir Denis Boyd Admiral Air and Rear Admiral M. S. Slattery Vice Controller (Air) and chief of Naval Equipment were passengers. The Fairey Swordfish, nicknamed ' The Stringbag' was the only aircraft to remain fully operational in it's original form on carriers throughout World War Two. It's activities had helped to sink or damage a great deal of enemy shipping, and it's most outstanding action came on the night of November 11th 1940 when twenty such planes made a notable contribution at the Battle of Taranto crippling the Italian Fleet and helping to reverse the balance of sea power in the Mediterranean. This was the Fleet Air Arm's finest hour. This last flight from an aircraft carrier was, therefore, a nostalgic occasion.

Not long before OCEAN set sail on her first commission in the Mediterranean the ship made Naval history off Spithead when she achieved the first landing of a pure jet aircraft, on an aircraft carrier under way. A claim had already been made in June 1944 by the United States Navy when a Ryan XFR 1 piston jet Fireball landed on the U.S.S Wake Island. However this was an emergency landing due to the partial failure of the piston engine and the landing had only been *boosted* by the jet unit. On 3rd December 1945, the Royal Navy intended to do it properly.

Under construction at Alexander Stephens yard. Linthouse. 1944

Trials on the Clyde 1945

The day was uninviting, a heavy swell causing the ship to pitch and roll. There were a large number of VIPs on board - R. E. Bishop, chief designer for De Havilland; the designers of the Hurricane and Spitfire, Sydney Camm and R. J. Mitchell; A. Woodburn, Parliamentary Secretary to the Ministry of Aircraft Production; and Sir Denis Boyd, the Fifth Sea Lord.   At one point there was an announcement that the plane would remain at the Ford airfield.   Finally permission was given and at 11.28am Lieutenant Commander E. ' Winkle' Brown landed the Vampire jet LZ55/G on the deck of H.M.S OCEAN.   Four landings and take offs took place that day, followed by a further eight on December 6th.   To quote Eric Brown's own memories of the flight "I was very conscious that the Royal Navy wanted to be the first Navy in the world to move into the jet age, and that the Americans had the same ambition, and were hot on our heels.   If anything went wrong we would lose the race and all the prestige that went with it.   It was up to me to get it right, not just for my own sake but for the sake of the whole Navy. With all this at stake I was very glad to hear that the trials carriers was to be OCEAN, for it was commanded by Captain Caspar-John, who had been my skipper when I was a pilot on the trials carrier PRETORIA CASTLE. We had developed a good understanding and he had seen me operate in many aircraft all sorts of weather conditions. This fact, together with his own desire as an aviator to make this a ' first' probably accounted for his decision to let me land on, when the boffins had advised against it because of the excessive movement of the flight deck". Thus the honour of the first deck landing of a true jet underway belonged fair and square to the Royal Navy and to H.M.S OCEAN.

A great deal of history was made on these two days in December and it is interesting to note that in recent years the LZ551/G has been restored by the Society of Friends of the Fleet Air Arm and it now holds pride of place on the flight deck of the ' Carrier' exhibition at the Fleet Air Arm Museum at Yeovilton in Somerset.

Squadron Workshops. First Commission 1945-46. Malta

De Havilland Sea Hornet trial. August 1945. Scotland

Hawker Sea Fury Trial. August 1945. Scotland

The last Swordfish flight from a British Carrier. October 1945.

HMS Ocean. As seen from the swordfish on its last Service Flight. October 1945

Vampire Jet. On board HMS Ocean. December 1945.

Pilot "Winkle Brown" taking off in Vampire Jet aircraft. December 1945.

The first pure Jet-Vampire LZ551/G lands on board HMS Ocean. 3rd december 1945.

Roughers in The Bay of Biscay. December 1945.

1946 - 1948

Night Flying, Corfu and Palestine

It was intended that OCEAN operate in the Far Eastern theatre of war, but peace was declared before the ship reached full complement. On VJ Day she anchored in Liverpool Bay for two days while the whole of the country celebrated the end of hostilities. Instead of heading for the Pacific, in mid December 1945 1792 squadron Fireflies and 892 squadron Hellcats were embarked from Macrahanish and OCEAN sailed from Greenock with her escort, the destroyer HMS MEYNELL, for Gibraltar. The wintry weather in the Bay of Biscay meant that speed was reduced to 10 knots, and the ship sustained damage caused by the high seas to the underside of the flight deck on the starboard side and to aircraft in the hangar. Christmas Day was spent in harbour at Gibraltar and the ship finally reached Malta on January 4th 1946.

Malta - The land of bells, smells, priests and nanny goats - was to be the home on and off for OCEAN and her ship's company for the next few years. One Able Seaman at that time recalls ' The Gut' . "It was still lively. A typical run ashore for the big ship men in Grand Harbour would commence in the 'Great War Bar', then up the steps to the ' Egyptian Queen' , on to the ' New Life' , and down the steps to the 'Bing Crosby' and others. A stop for ' big eats' was a must, and there was no doubt that most of the steak, with the two egg and chips, was horsemeat. After a run on Blue Label and Ambeet who cared? Floriana and the 'Klondyke' bar was a Sunday night adventure. Bobby, an accomplished 'gay' pianist played anything from Rachmaninov to Ragtime. Another called 'Mingo', billed as 'Miss Annabelle Lee', would provide a 'drag act' , -fairly crude but it went down well with the matelots. Sometimes the sailors would entertain themselves in the Fleet canteen at Corradino with 'Sod's Opera'."

On February 28th OCEAN set sail for Alexandria. There were signs of the rioting which had commenced on a serious level on March 1st when news was received that six people had been killed, two of them being British soldiers, and that one hundred and thirty had been injured. At Ras El Tin, where the Naval personnel were outnumbered, the Ensign had been torn down by the mob, the Quartermaster seized and paraded through the streets dressed as a 'Wog' and the Fleet Club set on fire. The local police and members of the Egyptian army soon brought calm to the storm, and the trouble died down

By March 5th the ship was on her way for exercises off Haifa and arrived at Cyprus two days later. (The ship's company had an opportunity to 'sample' the local strong brandy for the first time - four shillings a bottle). OCEAN then paid a visit to Suda Bay, Crete; a place of nostalgia for the Captain who had been Second in Command on board H.M.S YORK, but had left that ship shortly before it's demise in the bay in 1941, only months after the Battle of Taranto. Caspar John ordered a circuit of the area by OCEAN, in homage, before her return to base.

The ship's ability to operate night fighter aircraft gave her the distinction of being the only operational night carrier in the Fleet. During January to April, the first night flying exercises took place. A Wellington bomber set out from it's land base to act as an ' intruder' in the area. The ship's company closed up for night flying on the darkened carrier. Suddenly, two vivid lights, like jungle cat's eyes, broke the darkness - the exhausts of two Hellcats warming up. One was to take position over the ship and try to locate the intruder; the other was to make a lone trip to Syracuse to watch for ' enemy' ship movements.
-
The operations room was tense. Outlined on the screen were formations of cloud, and clearly recorded was the rugged coast of Malta. Suddenly the air was rent as the first Hellcat was waved off into the darkness, lurched along the deck; and with a roar pitched into the night sky. The ship had headed into the wind to give extra resistance for take off. The second took off with flames from the tail exhaust lighting up the deck as it swayed along the short runway. Over the next few hours planes took off and landed on a deck in darkness, picked out only by multi coloured lights and the batsman's direction. the ship still pitching on in the blackness, only the tell tale wake churning out behind her. By dawn all planes had returned safely - a successful exercise well done and without casualties.

Life was also difficult for the off-watch members of the general ship's company who were trying to sleep throughout the night. If your mess was one deck below the flight deck it could be quite frightening. The noise of the steam catapult and the roar of the engines on take off, the screech of the wheels and the grinding of the arrested wires as they caught the aircraft on landing. In contrast, the night squadron pilots found difficulty in adjusting to daytime sleep. During a four months period Fireflies of 1792 Squadron and Hellcats of 892 Squadron made 1100 day landings, and 250 night landings without serious accident. The latter was a tremendous feat considering operations were in complete darkness from the deck of a carrier under way.

In April , at the end of a four month work-up, OCEAN set sail for England. During this time many lessons had been learned. In particular the Captain commented on the deficiencies of the advanced radar for night flying operations that had been installed - the lack of steadiness at sea in rough weather was not satisfactory for landing and take off.

Arriving in Gibraltar on April 6th, six Wren officers and 1 VAD embarked for England (the first servicewomen to take passage in a warship). ' The Top Flight Honeys' , as they were known lived, in the Captain's day cabin and slept on mattresses on the floor, eating their meals in the wardroom to mixed approval by it's male members.

OCEAN arrived at Rosyth on April 16th after a very short first commission. Both squadrons had been flown ashore to be disbanded; 1792 under the command of Lieutenant Commander S. Dixon-Child RNVR, and 892 commanded by Major J. O. Armour R.M. (there were several very distinguished and successful Royal Marine officers serving as pilots in the Fleet Air Arm). Many of the ship's company also left the ship to be demobbed. Captain John had tried to persuade them to stay; but the war was over, many had been in the service right through World War Two and were more interested in finding a new life in civvy street than in continuing life at sea in peacetime.

After leave and replenishment OCEAN called at Portsmouth on June 19th to embark two new squadrons - 805 Seafires commanded by Lieutenant Commander P. Hutton and 816 Fireflies under the command of Lieutenant Commander J.S.L. Crabbe The ship set sail once more for Malta in mid July with H.M.S RAIDER taking over escort duties from MEYNELL. Once there she joined the Mediterranean Fleet for the Summer cruise visiting Tripoli , Rhodes and Crete.

These waters were also being patrolled for illegal immigrant ships sailing for Palestine. About 4, 500 people had been prevented by the Royal Navy from reaching their destination and had been placed in a camp just outside Famagusta, guarded by the King's Shropshire Light Infantry. An officer in charge was heard to remark that "they are uncouth, ill-mannered and in a filthy state - and of this number 198 are pregnant women' .

For four days from September 21st a little light relief came in the form of the Annual Fleet Regatta. This year H.M.Ships LIVERPOOL (the Flagship), LEANDER , MAURITIUS, OCEAN, PHOEBE and the R.F.A BLUE ANCHOR came together to 'do battle'. A Signalman at the time recalls it well. "The fleet at anchor was a sight to see. Each ship had it's team in the water for practice, which started at 7.30am and went on until mid afternoon. When one crew finished another took it's place. Officers, Seamen, Stokers, Signals, every branch joined in. Crew members not participating played a vital part by doing extra duties for their shipmates. The enthusiasm on the mess decks were tremendous. After each day's training was over the boats were hauled inboard (instead of onto the flight deck where they were normally serviced) to hide them from prying eyes on other ships, and wiped, rubbed down and polished. The general opinion that year was that our boats were not good, and these opinions were confirmed later. The Flag deck was never empty and questions abounded. 'What's LIVERPOOL like?' and 'What do you think of PHOEBE?' The answers were always the same. 'Very good' , so that the crews were not lulled into a sense of false security.

Usually the only gambling permitted on board was Tombola, but on the day of the regatta a table and blackboard were set up on the flight deck and the odds worked out. A bet could be placed on any boat on any ship. On that day dress regulations were relaxed, and the ship's company could wear civvies or fancy dress. Some of the more adventurous ratings had been known to address officers by their christian names (junior officers, of course). In 1946 OCEAN didn't win one race, a great disappointment to the Captain as well as the crew. H.M.S MAURITIUS was the winner hands and was proclaimed the ' Cock of the Fleet' , and in the late afternoon went around the fleet in an MFV displaying a large replica of a cockerel. The MFV gave each ship a very wide berth, though, because much ' stuff' was thrown at them. MAURITIUS then displayed the replica on their forward gun turret as she left the anchorage".

Captain Casper John(right) and Commander Nigel Henderson(left) 1946.

Loyalty to one's ship had been paramount and trophies had been fought for ferociously, but despite the disappointment keenly felt by OCEAN's ship's company it was agreed that a good day had been had by all.

On October 22nd, while OCEAN was in Greek waters and was engaged in flying exercises off Githian, Caspar John received a dramatic signal. A serious accident had occurred off the coast of Albania, only five miles away from Corfu, and help was needed to fight the fires and evacuate casualties. All aircraft were immediately recalled, and as soon as they had returned the ship steamed at 22 knots to find two destroyers, H.M.Ships SAUMAREZ and VOLAGE, caught up in a tragedy which had wrecked both ships. On 22nd October 1946, the two destroyers had been in company with the cruisers MAURITIUS and LEANDER, transiting the channel between Corfu and Albania. SAUMAREZ struck a mine, which severely damaged her (irreparably, as it turned out) and killed 36 of the crew. She was taken in tow by VOLAGE, and one and a half hours later VOLAGE also struck a mine, which blew off her bow and killed 8 crew members. She was, however, able to continue the tow over the bow while steaming astern.

H.M.S OCEAN finally arrived in sight of the two stricken ships at 21.00 hours to find fires still burning. Lieutenant Croome, an Air Engineer officer and a specialist in fighting fires at sea, led the first party of men from OCEAN to assist in fighting the fires still burning furiously onboard SAUMAREZ. They had to inch their way through blazing oil, foam, and at one point a cordite fire in a magazine which supplied a forward 4.7 inch gun, to tackle the blaze. By now the surrounding Naval vessels were working by the light of their searchlights. The battered destroyers desperately needed OCEAN's fully equipped hospital facilities, doctors and sick berth attendants. A Greek doctor and six assistants from Corfu helped to treat the injured, most of whom had burns. So many casualties were taken on board that the sick bay was filled to capacity and the quarter-deck was pressed into service to provide room for the less injured. The ship's crane swung into action to transfer the stretchers from the small boats to the flight deck. They were brought up on large drip trays, usually used beneath aircraft; and then on to trolleys designed to load up bombs. Members of the ship's company seized the stretchers as they arrived inboard and rushed them between parked aircraft and down the companionways to the appropriate areas. There was still time for humour - one badly burned seaman was heard to say to the Medical officer that "he had left the sunlamp on too long".

The rescue completed, twelve dead from the two destroyers were buried in the small British cemetery in Coloctronis Street in Corfu Town, taken in funeral procession through the streets and mourned by survivors of SAUMAREZ and VOLAGE and parties of sailors from the rescue ships. Thirty one bodies were never recovered from the sea and one rating (a cook) died on November 4th in hospital.

On October 25th, her duty done, OCEAN left Corfu with paravanes streamed, for Argustoli. The Corfu incident, as it came to be called, had been a terrible act of war in peacetime, showing the widening rift between Communist States and the Free World. Albanian shore batteries had shelled Royal Naval vessels on previous occasions and mines had been laid in the Corfu Channel only months before this event. On Tuesday December 30th the matter was brought to a Cabinet meeting at Downing Street by Ernest Bevin. He reported that "The Albanian reply to the British protest is completely unsatisfactory. It contains no response to the British demand for apologies or for compensation for the loss of 44 British lives and heavy damage to the two ships. The Albanian Government even goes so far to say that the two British ships had no right to be in the Corfu Channel where they struck the mines, though it is a waterway internationally recognised as a highway open to all ships at all times".

The International Court at the Hague later ruled that Albania *was* responsible and in London Gold Reserves from that country were frozen by the Bank of England against compensation. For all this justification, condemnation and eventual award by the International Court of £800, 000, the maimed and dependants of those killed never received a penny, Albania refused to accept responsibility.

On November 11th OCEAN returned to Corfu and Caspar John delivered one of his famous pep talks to the ship's company: "We are going back to sweep the sea around Corfu whether the Albanian's like it or not. Just off Corfu , outside the three mile limit, our cruisers are standing by to shell any guns ashore that might open fire on our minesweepers. Our aircraft will be up all day and the ship's company are warned that they might have to go to action stations at any time".

On November 13th the first part of the minefield was cleared, a path eight miles through the Corfu Gap. The role of 816 squadron , armed with 60 pound rocket projectiles capable of producing a punch as devastating as the broadside of a light cruiser should the necessity arise, was to patrol airspace over a number

Commander flying in Sea Otter being hoisted inboard 1946.

Hellcats (892) ranged ready for take off. Cyprus. 1946

Firefly (1792). Deck landing crash. Night Flight. 1946.

Flight Deck crane 1946.

HMS Ocean high and dry in the new floating dock which had been brought from Bombay in three sections. Malta 1946.

Sunday Divisions 1946. Nauplia

Visit of Gordon Highlanders pipe band. Tripoli. 1946.

Liberty Boat 1946.

Nauplia Bay. 1946. left hand Whaler Warrant Officers, right hand Whaler.
Communications.

of minesweepers trawling the channel off Saranda Bay to Denta Point until the Flotilla moved out into open sea. With eight aircraft constantly airborne out of a total of sixteen, this was no mean achievement. In the event, however, everything was so quiet that the requirement was eventually relaxed and on the following day the ship was able to return to Malta. Once there, Captain Caspar John relinquished command to Captain A. W. Clarke; enabling him to return to England to attend the Imperial Defence College. Lieutenant Commander S. 'Sammy' Hook took over command of 816 squadron in early January 1947.

After a period in Grand Harbour, OCEAN hoisted the flag of Vice Admiral Sir C J Harcourt, Flag Officer (Air) Mediterranean and second in command Mediterranean Fleet. On 28th January 1947 the ship set sail for a brief visit to Port Said. On the passage back to Malta, on February 7th, OCEAN shadowed two ships of the Italian Navy - ITALIA and VITTORIA VENETO - which had been interned in the Bitter Lakes. Their destination was Augusta, Sicily, where they were to be handed over to the Italian authorities under the terms of the Peace Treaty.

The Mediterranean fleet Spring Cruise followed, during which OCEAN visited Toulon, Leghorn and Rapallo (the first visits by British warships since World War Two). Toulon harbour was still full of wartime wreckage, Leghorn was still under the control of the U.S. Army. Some of the ship's company were fortunate enough to visit Rome, Assisi and Florence in cars loaned by the U.S. army complete with drivers. Rapallo was just a pleasant and picturesque coastal resort on the Italian Riviera, a nice place to relax. However a wartime reminder came on arrival at Rapallo when H.M.S. RAIDER, the escort destroyer, exploded a stray mine floating near OCEAN's hull. On completion of the visit the ship returned to Malta.

805 Squadron. 1946.
Back row. Ron Asplin,Ron Fowler,David Crofts,Phil Atterton
Middle row. Penny Penniston Bird,Pter Hiles,junior Turnbull,Jackie Ellis
Front row. Dave Hook,Tich Madden,Pete Hutton,Bill Gunner

816 Squadron at Lee on Solent. Spring 1946.
Sitting on wing. Ray Western, David Blair, Chuck Drake, Algy Groombridge, Bob Mills-
Goodlet? Vollmer, Jack Davis, Geoff Everett.
Standing. Teddy Genge, Tony Atkins, Ricky Neville Jones, Johnny Crabb, Buck Buchan-
Sydserff, Ray Hastie, Ian Keddie Clarke, Fiskwick, Dave ffiske.

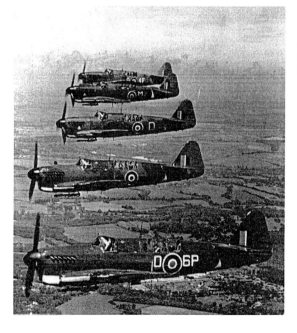

Some of 816 Squadron
over Lee on Solent prior
to landing on HMS
Ocean. 1946.

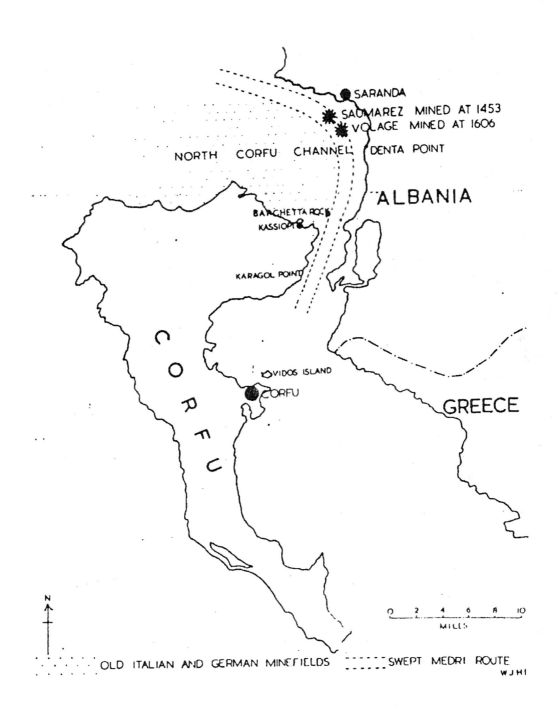

SARANDA

SAUMAREZ MINED AT 1453

VOLAGE MINED AT 1606

NORTH CORFU CHANNEL   DENTA POINT

ALBANIA

BARCHETTA ROCK

KASSIOPI

KARAGOL POINT

VIDOS ISLAND

CORFU

GREECE

C O R F U

N

0   2   4   6   8   10
MILES

OLD ITALIAN AND GERMAN MINEFIELDS   SWEPT MEDRI ROUTE

W J H I

HMS Ocean, - Sons of the Desert

HMS OCEAN
CHRISTMAS 1946

'SOME HA' MEAT AND CANNA EAT, SOME THERE BE
THAT WANT IT,
BUT WE HA' MEAT AND WE CAN EAT
AND SO THE LORD BE THANKIT'

MENU

BREAKFAST
PORRIDGE
EGG & BACON
MARMALADE & ROLLS

DINNER
CREAM OF TOMATO SOUP
ROAST TURKEY   BOILED HAM
SAUSAGE MEAT STUFFING
ROAST POTATOES
BOILED CAULIFLOWER & GREEN PEAS
CHRISTMAS PUDDING
BRANDY SAUCE

TEA
CHRISTMAS CAKE
FRUIT SALAD & JELLY

SUPPER
SOUP
COLD ROAST PORK
PICKLES & FRESH SALAD
MINCE PIES

ORANGES   NUTS   APPLES

ORANGE & LEMON CRYSTALS

Christmas menu

816 Squadron, May 1947.

Back row. Lt Davey,Lt Lang,S/Lt Hill, Lt Grant, Lt Mills-Grooglett, Lt Groombridge, S/Lt Fillingham, Lt Hutton, S/Lt Black.
Centre row. S/Lt Carter, S/Lt Nevill-Jones, S/Lt Blair, S/Lt Williams, S/Lt Gilman, Lt Western, S/Lt Swithinbank, S/Lt Everett, S/Lt Sear, Lt Woodland.
Front row. Lt Manuel, Lt Hanks, Lt Lobb, Lt Genge, Lt Gore-Langton, Lt Cdr Hook, Lt Lee-White, Lt Holme, Lt Buchan-Sydorrf, Lt Gunther

Firefly I's of 816 Squadron over Malta. 1947

HMS Volage in Malta Dockyard December 1946.

HMS Saumarez off the coast of Albania. October 1946.

816 Squadron Pilots and Maintenance Crew. 1947

In mid 1947 the Fleet was ordered to proceed to the Aegean Sea where each ship was to lay at anchor off the islands, singly. There had been an outbreak of suspected polio and a quarantine imposed. OCEAN had been allotted a Sea otter to comprise a communications flight, for the transporting of patients, stores and mail between the ship and Athens, and ship to ship, flying all the hours of daylight for the period of isolation (about 2 weeks).

A short visit to Tripoli in mid June preceded OCEAN's deployment on the Summer cruise. The squadrons made a seven day visit to R.A.F. Castel Benito in late May. The squadrons (805 and 816) formed the 20th Carrier Air Group under the command of Lieutenant Commander J.S. Crabb.

During the Summer cruise OCEAN took passage to Istanbul, a memorable visit and once again the first for a warship since World War Two. The visit was capped when the ship passed through the Bosphorus into the Black Sea, an area where a previous OCEAN was mined and sunk in 1915. The Regatta was, as usual, at Nauplia and then followed a visit to Larnaca before the ship returned to Malta. Lieutenant Commander P.E.I. Bailey assumed command of 805 squadron in September. In the autumn OCEAN made visits to Aranci Bay, Famagusta and Beirut interspersed by several exercises in the area of Palestine, the last being in early November. Outside Haifa the ship was involved in stopping and boarding at least one immigrant ship which was then escorted to Cyprus for internment. The ship also practised gunnery spotting and bombardment while 805 squadron Seafires exercised patrolling the roads leading to Haifa. The ship's squadrons worked with the Middle East School of Artillery which embarked some of their Auster aircraft. By the end of November OCEAN was back in Malta once more and entered dry dock for a refit.

During the early months of 1948 OCEAN was involved in flying exercises. To quote Peter Hiles, a pilot of 805 squadron "We embarked in OCEAN again on January 15th and, at first, both squadrons did a lot of cross operating with H.M.S TRIUMPH to see how many aircraft could be safely operated on a light fleet carrier. We got up to 38 on deck for take-off. I remember following the C.O. for a free take-off (no catapult) from just forward of the island superstructure - staggering was hardly the word for it."

The ship also spent quite a lot of time in Grand Harbour. A boy seaman remembers becoming a messenger, mostly on the bridge or compass platform at sea, and the early morning exercises looking out over the wide empty circle of the sea, more often than not breathing in the sulphur fumes from the funnel. In harbour he helped to paint the black band at the ship's waterline. Sometimes the passing launches made the platform unsteady, resulting in the painting party having to swim back to the gangway. Spare time was spent in Valletta, where ' Jack' was ripped off to a greater or lesser degree depending on how drunk he was, and was very often attended by the ' percentage girls' . Often certain bars became the sole domain of a particular ship, and woe betide anyone from another ship who tried to enter. In consequence there were many punch-ups between the different ships' companies. By late evening the ' Gut' would be one long fighting, singing, swearing, and spewing heaving mass of bluejackets, on which the shore patrols and Maltese police would descend. Those who were not too overcome would then fade into the night, back to the their ships - leaving others to the shore patrols and the inevitable appearance at defaulters in the morning. All this, of course, was in great contrast to the Naval Officers Club at St. Pauls Bay where you could have dinner for 1/6d and a bottle of wine for 10d old money.

On some nights there was also a film onboard. One of the hangar fire curtains would be dropped and the film projected on it, while the ' patrons' sat on chairs in the lift well. One night, while they were all enjoying the film, some bright spark on the flight deck decided to send the lift down. As the bell (which warned that the lift was descending) began to ring, all hell broke lose. Everyone tried to get out to safety, and with a hundred or so bods, and their chairs, on the move it looked like a scene from the ' Keystone Cops' .

The Spring Cruise in 1948, in February and March, took in Algiers, San Tropez, and Corsica. Then on May 7th the squadrons were re-embarked and OCEAN sailed once again for Palestine, this time to cover the hand over to Israeli authorities at the end of British rule on May 31st . OCEAN's role was to cruise off the coast and fly patrols to help cover the withdrawal of the army during the final days. A large number of vehicles and many troops were taken on board, the soldiers bedding down on the hanger deck. There was tight security on stores at the jetty. Potatoes for instance were completely emptied from their sacks for inspection before being brought from the mainland. Parcels brought on board by any of the ships company were opened in front of the O.O.W. on the gangway, and civilians were not allowed into the ship's boats until their parcels had been opened and inspected by the Midshipman or

Seafire XVII's of 805 Squadron. Over Malta 1947.

20th Carrier Air Group (816 and 805 Squadrons) during summer cruise 1947.

Football Team 1946-1948

Back Row. C Murray P and RTI, L Townsend RM, W Ayerst ST(m) NV Hodgson LT(a)

Middle row. P King OA, L Davies ST(m), M Cole SPO(m), W Munro LCK, E Fidler AM, T Smale (ST(m), T Seager EMI

Front row. Lt CDR J W B Bennett, R Wakeford PO.CK, Captain A W Clarke DSO, Lt CDR L G Toone, J Weight SHPT, J Harrison P.O.

Cross legged. J Bennett AB, W Smith O/SEA

Winners Med Fleet KO Shield competion 1946-47
Winners Group 1 League Cup 1947-48
Finalists inter Group Competion 1947-48

216 Crashes in the MED 1947.

Air Crew briefing 1947

Army Auster, Palestine 1948. It landed in ten yards.

Well done chef

Divine Service in the hanger.

Coxswain of the boat. Private boats were not allowed within 20 yards of the ship day or night and a hose was kept rigged at gangways for use if verbal orders were not obeyed.

At the end of April Captain ' Nobby' Clarke was succeeded in command by Captain W.R.C Leggatt .

On May 14th came the final departure of the British High Commissioner, His Excellency General Sir Alan Cunningham; the elder brother of Admiral of the Fleet Lord Cunningham.   The Commissioner boarded H.M.S EURYALUS which was escorted by ships including OCEAN to the last point of His Excellency's jurisdiction - the three mile limit - at midnight on May 14th/15th. EURYALUS passed close to OCEAN so that a last goodbye could be said in Naval fashion, all ships floodlit and Guard and Band (including pipers from the 1st Bn Irish Guards)paraded on the flight deck. A salute was fired and British rule in Palestine was at an end.

On the following day a message was sent to all ships, "The Navy has done the last British High Commissioner for Palestine proud and has maintained on leaving the high prestige which Britain has always maintained in the country." OCEAN also received a signal from the Flag Officer (Air) Med., "Arrangements made for the send off of the High Commissioner for Palestine were very well carried out by the 20th CAG and H.M.S OCEAN. I was particularly gratified by the good turnout of the ship's company at midnight and feel certain that the ceremony, as was intended, will leave a lasting impression in the mind of General Sir Alan Cunningham." The pipers were also thanked for their faultless and impressive display on OCEAN's flight deck.

Now that the duty in Palestine was completed, the Captain made this signal:-

"Today and tonight we have probably seen the last deck landings of the 20th Carrier Air Group aboard H.M.S OCEAN. I for one will always be indebted to them for their impressive display which clearly showed a high standard of team work and all round efficiency. Now officers and men of the Group have finished their period of operational flying and I am sure that all in H.M.S OCEAN will wish them continued success in their new job. Yet you will find the airmen the first to pay tribute to the boys below decks - the engineers, stokers and mechanics, the highly skilled radio and radar teams and others concerned in the general running of the ship - without them no carrier could be operated successfully."

Ocean returned to Malta, full to overflowing with the embarked army personnel together with their trucks, equipment, and several Auster aircraft on the flight deck. They had served in a thankless task, maintaining law and order over a long period and trying to prevent open war in a very unruly and dangerous situation.

In mid-June 1948 OCEAN turned her bows for home after a two year commission in the Mediterranean. On arrival at her home port, the 20th C.A.G. was disbanded on 1st July, 816 squadron at Lee on Solent and 805 squadron at Eglington

The British High Commissioner leaves Palestine. May 1948

Cruising, Trooping and Quarantine

After leave and replenishment the ship sailed to work up in the South Western approaches followed by a week alongside at Portsmouth before returning to Malta in August. Twelve Firefly MK5's of 812 squadron were flown on under the command of Lieutenant Commander F.G.B. Sheffield. The squadron was supplemented by four Firefly NFI's (Black Flight) which had been left behind at Hal Far when 816 squadron had returned to England. Thirteen Seafire FR47's of 804 squadron also embarked, commanded by Lieutenant Commander SFF Shotton, and later by Lieutenant Commander R. N. Hargreaves from February 1949. These two squadrons made up the 14th C.A.G.

From November OCEAN took part in exercises with the U.S. Sixth Fleet and on completion sailed through the Straits of Messina to visit Naples. The ship passed the island of Stromboli, on which the volcano was very active, at night and the ship's company had a spectacular view of the lava flow. A spot of shore leave in Naples brought out at least one entrepreneur on board. Lieutenant Owen recalls "Able Seaman Cash was quite talented musically and played the Mandolin. In Naples he made a few Lira whilst playing outside the San Paolo Opera House - for extra beer money"

Early in the new year the ship entered dry-dock in Malta for two months, and on March 28th 1950 she was transferred to no. 8 buoy in Grand Harbour. During this period Lieutenant Commander R. M. Fell succeeded Lieutenant Commander Sheffield as Commanding Officer of 812 squadron. On April 12th the squadrons embarked from Hal Far to take part in the Spring cruise. On the 29th OCEAN arrived in Venice and a ' pinwheel' was carried out in the lagoon, From there she proceeded to Trieste, arriving on May 6th. The city was still governed by a tripartite military system, divided into an American, British and Yugoslav zone – the latter being Iron Curtain territory. There were limited runs ashore, and a ship's company dance was held in the British zone.

On June 20th the Summer cruise was cancelled and the two squadrons of the 14th C.A.G. were flown off to Hal Far to await H.M.S GLORY from the UK; OCEAN was withdrawn from the Mediterranean and sailed for Devonport.

Captain Clarke rowed ashore by his fellow Officers 1948.

St Tropez. 1948

Ships company and "Beauties" entertain. 1948

In early July she was again underway, and reached Glasgow KGV dock on July 7th to load an R.A.F. squadron of about seventy Typhoon and Tempest aircraft (the wings detached for storage) and spares. The hanger and flight deck were filled to capacity when OCEAN sailed to Portsmouth to embark the R.A.F. personnel. On completion of loading OCEAN departed for the Mediterranean and passage through the Suez Canal to Aden and her destination, Hong Kong. Stoker Mechanic Hackett remembers that " Our passage through the canal came to a grinding halt because we were so low in the water that our main engine condensers topped up with sand. After clearing out we were towed a few miles until we could once again make our own way"
Half of the aircraft were unloaded at Singapore for the Malayan Campaign, and the rest at Hong Kong on August 14th.

By 1950 Communism was firmly in control North of the 38th parallel in Korea. Soviet troops had been withdrawn by the end of 1948 and by July 1949 the United States withdrew the last of her troops except for a small team of advisers. Despite an attempt by a U.S. Commission to unite the two halves of the country in peaceful reunification, the first hot conflict in the Cold War between Communism and Capitalism came to a head on June 24th 1950 when North Korean troops invaded the South. A second resolution on June 27th requested U.N. members to assist South Korea to repel aggression and to restore peace to the area. By June 30th the North Korean Peoples Army had occupied Seoul and a large force had landed at Kangmung and Samchuk. From that date large numbers of American troops, acting on United Nations orders, began to back up the South Koreans. Within three days many countries had offered assistance; the Canadian, Australian and New Zealand governments had pledged Naval support and the Australians air support from their R.A.A.F. squadrons based at Iwakkuni in Japan. President Harry Truman ordered U.S. air and sea forces including the U.S. 7th Fleet to give the South Koreans support; and Clement Atlee the British Prime Minister pledged his government's help to the South Koreans to resist aggression. General MacArthur became Commander-in-Chief, United Nations Forces. In August the Communist advance was halted near Taegu and during September and October combined U.N. troops broke out of their foothold around Pusan. Amphibious landings at Inchon and Woonsan threw the North Koreans into confusion and pushed them back to the Yalu River.

H.M.S TRIUMPH, with 800 and 827 Squadrons embarked and H.M.S COSSACK as escort, sailed from Kure on June 29th 1950 for the West coast of Korea and the Yellow Sea arriving at the beginning of July. TRIUMPH was to remain in the area until September 29th, to be replaced by H.M.S THESEUS, with 807 and 810 squadrons embarked, from Hong Kong until April 23rd 1951. In turn H.M.S GLORY took position with 804 and 812 squadrons until September 1951.

Meanwhile, in mid April 1950 OCEAN sailed for the Far East on a further trooping mission under the command of Captain B.E.W. Logan, transiting the Mediterranean and the Canal to Aden and stopping off at Trincomalee, Singapore and Hong Kong. The 3rd Commando Brigade had been in Hong Kong since 1949 as part of the reinforcements to the Island and the New Territories. On May 25th a large contingent of Royal Marines from 40, 42 and 45 commando units boarded OCEAN for passage home. One of that number, Brian Tinnion remembers it well. "We had been told that the ship was on a trooping voyage - it was to last until July 5th. Later we were told that the journey would last for 'maybe six weeks'. From Hong Kong OCEAN sailed for Kure in Japan where the ship delivered and also embarked various items of cargo. Whilst there we were surprised to awake one morning to notice Japanese shipyard workers, suspended on wooden working platforms, applying a new coat of paint; indeed the whole ship on the outside was given the brush treatment. There were several other aircraft carriers in Kure, at least four, and it was not until, later that we realised the reason for their presence - with British involvement the Korean War was really about to commence. On the return journey, at Singapore, an old Rolls Royce - an open tourer circa 1920's was taken aboard. You can imagine the attention it attracted when it was lowered from the ship when we reached Portsmouth. OCEAN finally reached Plymouth on July 25th and we Marines disembarked to Stonehouse Barracks - and sixty days leave."

On August 1st Captain R. C. Versey-Ross took over command from Captain Logan for the last trooping of the year to the East, calling at Colombo and Hong Kong on route, and reaching Sasebo on October 18th to secure at no. 19 buoy. On the return journey OCEAN called in to Trincomalee instead of Colombo and then headed for home calling at Malta to embark stores, 119 ratings and 1 Sergeant R.M. for passage to the U.K. By December 12th OCEAN was anchored off the Breakwater, Plymouth and preparing for an extensive refit.

In early June 1951 OCEAN came out of dry dock at Rosyth , extensively refitted and refurbished. Captain C L G Evans became the new Commanding Officer. This was a unique appointment, a World War

Two pilot credited with the destruction of sixteen enemy planes and the first aviator to command an aircraft carrier. This proved to be a fruitful appointment and within the next eighteen months the ship, under Captain ' Crash' Evans, was to smash almost every aviation record held by light Fleet Carriers.

On July 1st the Right Reverend Brian Burroughs, Bishop of St Andrews, rededicated the ship's Chapel of St Peter, and on July 16th she left the basin to secure at a buoy in the Firth of Forth. The ship's company embarked ready for the squadrons to be flown on 807 squadron Sea Fury FB11's under the command of Lieutenant Commander A J Thompson and 898 squadron Sea Fury FB11's commanded by Lieutenant Commander T L M Brander made up the 17th C.A.G. By the 26th July the ship was anchored off Portland to embark provisions and stores.

On July 27th OCEAN set sail for the Med. accompanied by the escort destroyer H.M.S SAINTES and arrived in Malta on August 3rd. On the 21st there were reports of a Polio epidemic on the island in 'The Times of Malta'. Within a few days three members of the ship's company from OCEAN were in hospital as suspect cases and as a precautionary measure the ship sailed from Grand Harbour flying the yellow quarantine flag and put into Marsaxlokk Bay for the next fourteen days. Two days later H.M.C.S MAGNIFICENT (nicknamed the ' Maggie Ann') joined her at an adjacent buoy.

Despite all the difficulties encountered, the flying programme was not interrupted. Squadrons were still exercised, operating from Hal Far. Aircrew landing on were segregated, remaining on deck during inactive periods, and dining alone.

Boredom of the ship's company was of great concern and team competitions were instituted between every mess - darts, whist, uckers, cribbage, swimming, water polo, deck cricket and hockey being among the activities encouraged. There were occasional Banyan parties on an isolated beach complete with beer bar. At night the ' Polio Stakes' were run on a miniature race course constructed on the flight deck. James Richard remembers "An ordinary dice game with horses moved over numbered squares, but all on a large scale. Each horse having it's own jockey who moved the horse according to the throw of an enormous dice. Part of it's success were the members of the ship's company dressed up as bookies, tipster, hangers on, Hindu beggars, Negro witch doctors, doddering old colonels and tipsy clergymen . There was even a melancholy sandwich man calling down the wrath of God on this sinful carry on." The opening night was graced by Commander Hayes clad in the latest spring fashion as Lady Bountiful, rising from the after lift-well like Venus from the waves to be greeted by a massed barrage of rockets and Verey lights. Riding a flight deck bumper car "she" circumnavigated the entire flight deck en-route to the "race course".

The highlight of the fortnight was the ship's concert, appropriately called the ' Quarantine Follies'. Entertainment included the Polio Sisters, (shades of the famous American Andrews Sisters) - except that these were the Navigating officer, his Assistant (W) and the Captain of the Royal Marines, all giving a fair imitation of feminine beauty, - but one sporting a ginger moustache. A ballad on the merits of Fishheads and Pin-heads was sung by the Commander, saucy stories related by Lieutenant Gordon Dixon and harmonica solos by Stoker Bungy Williams.

One morning during this period of isolation ' CANADA FOREVER' was discovered to have been written on the starboard side in red lead paint. In retaliation OCEAN's Royal Marines pinched a Maple leaf motif from MAGNIFICENT, and as far as is known it was never returned. Fourteen days after initial quarantine the ship was given the green light to return to Grand Harbour. The epidemic had been contained.

On September 24th OCEAN sailed for the Autumn cruise with the Fleet. Arriving at the Naval base at La Spezia, tours were arranged for the ship's company to visit Milan, Florence, Pisa and also a visit to the Vatican by 42 officers and ratings for an audience with his Holiness The Pope.

On October 2nd the ship sailed once more to rendezvous with the Fleet, which included two French cruisers GLOIRE and GEORGE LEGUES, for exercises at St Raphael. On October 10th more than thirty warships formed up off Golfe Juan promontory before dispersal. OCEAN sailed for Malta on the 15th, with H.M.S CHEVIOT as escort, in a force eight gale. OCEAN's flight and weather decks were put out of bounds, a 32ft motor cutter was torn bodily from its stowage, and the boat snapped like a matchstick causing casualties who were treated in the heaving sick-bay. Two days later, with the sea still running high, OCEAN nosed her way into Grand Harbour.

In November the ship sailed for Tobruk escorted by H.M.S AISNE and H.M.S JUTLAND to meet up with H.M.S LIVERPOOL and H.M.S MERMAID for exercises with army troops ashore, and after a short period at Tripoli returned to Malta and to celebrate Christmas. A junior member of the ship's company remembers sitting on the flight deck on a Sea Fury chock after his Christmas dinner, taking in the view of Grand Harbour - not another soul around. Then Captain Evans joined him, sitting on the other wheel chock, and for several minutes chatted about life on board. Then they parted, the Captain of the ship and the Stoker Mechanic wishing one another Merry Christmas and Happy New Year.

On January 25th 1952 the ship left for Cyprus as a task force stand by in case needed. In Egypt and the Canal Zone riots had broken out. Several clubs, Barclays Bank and Sheppeard Hotel had been burnt down; many British nationals had been killed and damage had been estimated at £50,000. Fortunately the Egyptian Army were able to diffuse the situation. On February 12th OCEAN sailed to meet H.M.S THESEUS and exchange squadrons. February and March were spent working up the new squadrons, 802 Sea Furys and 825 Fireflys. The ship also spent a short time in dry dock, the progress of work almost marred by a threatened strike of dock workers in early March. By the beginning of April OCEAN, a clean ship in good condition, with two well exercised squadrons, was ready to sail for the Far East.

HMS Ocean in dry dock. Malta.

Sunbathing. Palestine 1948.

Final take-off of 20th CAG 1948.

Catapult trials-English Channel. Avenger taking off 29th August 1948.

Glasgow 1948

Towards the Rising Sun and the Korean War

Shortly before 9 am on Saturday April 5th 1952 the cable was slipped at no 7 buoy and H.M.S OCEAN was under way for Korea; the flight deck manned by the Ship's Company, the dark colour of their uniforms relieved by the red, white and blue of the Royal Marine Guard. In the gardens at the top of the Barraca Lift the wives and families gathered to wave goodbye and as the ' Still' was sounded the Captain gave a farewell salute to the Commander-in-Chief, Sir John Edelston, at Lascaris and also to the Flag Officer Malta in H.M.S St. ANGELO. Standing on the jetty was the Pipe Band of the Highland Light Infantry resplendent in their kilted uniform. As the ship steamed past they played ' Wings over the Navy' and ' Will ye no come back again' . The last tribute was paid by the Flag Officer, Second in Command, in person, as he stood with his family at the end of the breakwater. As the ship rendezvoused with the destroyer H.M.S St. KITTS, three Mosquito aircraft of the Royal Air Force flew over the ship in close formation, followed by a fourth towing a banner with the words GOODBYE, GOOD LUCK.

After two days sailing OCEAN reached the Suez Canal. The riot situation had died down with little noticeable evidence of the troubles save for a number of wrecked trains alongside the Suez to Cairo railway and a number of patrol vehicles. As the ship passed the camp of the Sussex Regiment the Royal Marine Band played the march ' Sussex by the Sea' , which was received by the army personnel ashore with good humour. At Port Tewfik the destroyer H.M.S. St. JAMES was sighted, occupied on guard duty, stationed close to the large memorial stone which dominates the Suez entrance to the canal. H.M.S St. KITTS relinquished her period of escort duty at Aden and OCEAN rendezvoused with her replacement H.M.S COMUS off Colombo and continued on to Singapore.

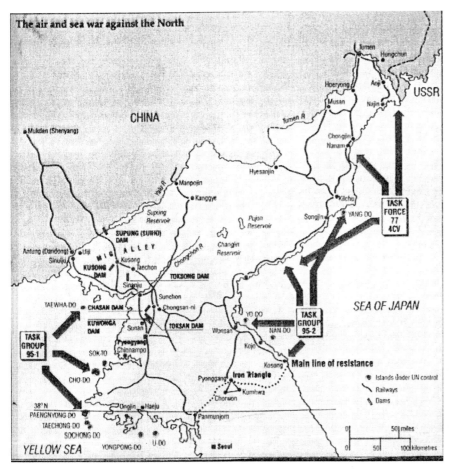

On leaving Singapore for passage to Hong Kong aircrew were briefed to assist with attacks on jungle villages on the Malay Peninsular known to be communist strongholds. Over 40 sorties were flown, a good rehearsal for the squadrons duties once they reached Korea OCEAN reached Hong Kong on April 30th to find H.M.S GLORY waiting to turn over her duties. The ships somewhat ancient Sea Otter was transferred to GLORY who in turn transferred her two Westland Sikorski Dragon Fly 551 helicopters. By May 6th OCEAN had sailed for Japan on the last leg of the journey to the was zone escorted by H.M.A.S WARRAMUNGA, and she arrived in Sasebo, the advanced United Nations Naval Base on May 9th. For the next two years GLORY, OCEAN and H.M.A.S SYDNEY had the task of patrolling a static war off the West coast of Korea.

HMS Ocean tied up at the refuelling buoy Aden, 1949

Wingless Typhoons on deck transported to Hong Kong with RAF personnel 1949.

"Bats" in action 1949.

Firefly being floated ashore to Kalafrana 1949

Off loading Firefly for Kalafrana workshop, 1949.

Pilot rescue at the second barrier, 1949.

Flag Officer (MED)(AIR) inspection. Malta 1949.

HMS Ocean with HMS Liverpool and HMS Gambia. Malta 1951. Crown Copyright

"The Polio Stakes"
Entertainment on board during quar-
antine in August 1951.

On the following day OCEAN sailed for her first patrol off the West coast of Korea - to point Oboe, a point on the chart most convenient for air operations by the Sea Furys of 802 squadron and the Fireflys of 825 squadron. Before arrival in Korea 802 had experience a great deal of trouble with the fuel tanks, caused by the deterioration of the self sealing compound. This fault was finally rectified by replacing the tanks.

A close blockade of the enemy coast was being maintained and the supplies harassed from the air. The blockade was divided between two commands with the East coast under the jurisdiction of the American Navy and the West coast under Flag Officer, Second in Command, Far East Fleet. H.M.S OCEAN's role was that of harassing enemy supplies, providing air support for troops of the British Commonwealth Division in the front line, and 'busting' bridges, radio stations, trains, supply dumps and even ox-carts which carried arms supplies to enemy groups.

During this period Captain Charles Evans was always looking for bigger and better ways of hitting the enemy and he discovered that some 1, 000 lb bombs could be obtained from Australian sources. The snag was that the Sea Fury could not get off the deck of the carrier with 2 x 1, 000 lb bombs - the normal load was 2 x 500 lb bombs in addition to the normal weapon load. However with Rocket Assisted Take off Gear (RATOG) the aircraft could be ' fired' into the air with the 1, 000lb bomb load. The aircrew had done some practice ' firings' from the runway at Hal Far, Malta, but no one really liked it. Nevertheless the decision was taken and all the firing circuits and equipment were carefully checked and rechecked. The Air Engineer Officer of the Sea Fury Squadron remembers "The morning dawned when it was to be used for the first time and the 802 squadron Commanding Officer Lieutenant Commander Fraser - Shotton, decided that honour would be served if he went off first. The aircraft roared down the deck, came opposite the point in the deck (marked by a flag) when the RATOG had to be fired, and nothing happened. The aircraft disappeared over the bows of the flight deck; all those watching were convinced that the aircraft had ditched in the sea ahead of the ship. You can imagine what the pilots in the cockpits of the aircraft in the range waiting to take off were thinking. Also technicians in the ground crews and armourers who were wondering if they had done something wrong or there was a defect in the rockets.

Suddenly, ahead of the ship, with it's tail almost touching the water, appeared a Sea Fury - staggering along. It slowly climbed away and the voice of the C.O. came over the R.T - "I forgot to make my masterswitch". What a relief on everyone's faces". And what a credit to the very popular C.O. to admit that it was his mistake. The lesson was learned, and from then on the Sea Furies went on to inflict extensive damage with the enhanced bombload and the assistance of RATOG.

On the first patrol, on May 17th, the squadron aircrews were all set to break the existing record of 106 sorties in a day achieved by H.M.S GLORY. By the end of the day, in a concerted effort, 802 squadron had flown 76 and 825 squadron 47 sorties. A brilliant result, with 28 out of 31 aircraft still serviceable.

Captain ' Crash' Evans sent this signal to the ship's company: "Our pilots have today broken all existing records for British Light Carriers in flying 123 sorties over our operating area. From dawn to dusk the area has been pounded by rocket and bomb attacks. The destruction figures include three bridges downed, four gun emplacements shattered, fifteen ammo laden ox-carts exploded and an oil fuel dump fired. Smoke and flames have been billowing from this for most of the day. The airspot for BELFAST scored a direct hit on a coastal battery with six inch salvoes. A total of 456 rockets, 72 bombs and 20, 300 rounds of ammunition have been consumed. Serviceability has remained excellent and we will continue with 68 sorties tomorrow".

A signal was received from Rear Admiral Dyer, U.S.N. commanding the task force: "The unprecedented record set by OCEAN evokes pride and admiration in us all. This is the kind of warfare by the U.N. which the Communists do not mention in the truce negotiations. Aggressiveness and top drawer training of pilots, ground crew and ships company reflected in your operations are noted with profound pleasure. To the Commanding Officer and each man of the OCEAN and her squadrons Rear Admiral George C Dyer sends WELL DONE."

From the Flag Officer, Second in Command Far East Station: " My best congratulations on your 123 sorties. A magnificent effort which indicates a highly worked up ship. I am only sorry I was not on board to witness this great feat."

OCEAN's two squadrons were fully occupied during the patrols. Some of the bridges were knocked down many times, but the enemy were good bridge builders and seemed to be able to repair a bridge overnight. Flak in most air operations was pretty heavy and many aircraft were hit by rifle fire whilst flying low to hit their targets. Ox-carts, one of the main ways of carrying troops and ammunition were hit constantly - but the North Koreans had a quick release system to free the oxen from their shafts and it was amazing how many animals got away. Transformer stations were also hit, and there was also air support for guerrilla landings; not always successful because of the slow junks used for transport. One such incident occurred on June 1st. OCEAN's two squadrons were engaged as a support group for ' Operation Billhook' which involved the landing of UN guerrillas landed near the Han River. H.M.S AMETHYST, the British frigate of Yangtse River fame, and the controlling ship for this operation, celebrated the Navy's Glorious First of June anniversary with a daring raid up the Han River, to direct a shore assault by allied junks. The AMETHYST's four inch guns first blazed at dawn to 'soften up' strong Chinese defences. The junk fleet, sheltering behind the rocky islets, hoisted sail and made for the landing beach, but the lack of wind held them up and gave the Chinese time to prepare. They turned intense crossfire and bombardment on the U.N. guerrillas as they advanced over the mud flats. Broadsides from AMETHYST kept the beach head under continual fire and Sea Fury fighters from OCEAN swept in with 500 pound bombs followed by Fireflys with rockets. Opposition proved heavy, though, and AMETHYST signalled ' Abandon Operation' after four hours. Her Commanding Officer, Captain A.R.L. Butter radioed OCEAN: "Thank you for air support which undoubtedly prevented complete disaster." OCEAN signalled back: "Hope to be present at the return match." The Captain of H.M.A.S BATAAN , Commander W.S. Bracegirdle, R.A.N. of Sydney, signalled to OCEAN: "On this first day of June it is evident the Royal navy has lost none of the sting in it's tail" OCEAN replied: "Thank You. As in Lord Howe's day the small ships are the backbone of the Fleet".

June 1st is the anniversary of Admiral Lord Howe's rout of the French. west of Ushant in 1794 and commemorated in one of OCEAN's battle honours.

There were, of course many hazards for the squadron pilots in those early days in the war zone. On the first patrol, on May 14th Lieutenant (E) K. McDonald of 802 was shot down and killed whilst on TAR-CAP, (Tactical Air Reconnaissance and Combat Air Patrol) just before attacking a gun position. On May 19th Lieutenant Commander T.J.C. Williamson Napier, senior pilot of 825, and his observer aircrewman L.M. Edwards were shot down by Anti-Aircraft fire. On July 4th, Lieutenant R. C. Hunter, Senior pilot 825 took off with his observer Lieutenant J.R.A. Taylor on a test flight. The engine failed almost immediately and forced him to ditch within sight of the ship. A helicopter was sent out, but could only pick the up one at a time, It returned to the ship with Taylor, and immediately when back to the place where the aircraft had ditched but after a vigorous search was unable to find the pilot. The last casualty on this first commission was Lieutenant Commander R. A. Dick who died on July 24th. He failed to recover from a dive on this target. The pilot had only just succeeded Lieutenant Commander Shotton as C.O. of 802 squadron (on July 13th), and now, in turn had to be replaced by Lieutenant Commander P.H. London on August 14th. It was a most unsettling period for both squadrons.

In addition to the air crew loss in these early days there were several other fatalities. On May 19th Naval Airman Herbert was killed on duty as port chockman, blasted over the side when a Sea Fury rocket battery fired when the plane was still in the range. His body was never recovered. On July 29th PO/REM R. P .Jordan walked into the rotating propeller of a Sea Fury he was maintaining at the time. There was only one more name of the fatality list during OCEAN's first deployment in Korea - that of A. Findlay, S.B.A, who died on June 4th.

With time and experience things settled down and there were no more deaths to add to the list during the rest of the ten patrols. However many aircraft were fired on or damaged in future incidents at a pretty heavy rate.

Lieutenant Derek 'Pug' Mather, an engineer, joined 802 squadron straight after pilot training. "On my 38th trip I was doing a combined test flight and CAP, and I had to force land on a beach on the island of Panyong. I was rescued by a chopper from on board OCEAN. Then, on the next day whilst on a pre dawn strike - RATOG take off - bombing mission and armed reconnaissance, I was flying low, attacking road transport, some infantry troops shot at me with rifles and a bullet severed my main fuel line. I had to force land in a paddy field near the coast north of Chinnampo. After about an hour, sitting on a wing, being looked after by a RESCAP, who kept the enemy troops away from the aircraft, a chopper (USAF) rescued me just in time and I was taken to the Island of Chodo. From there I was transferred to a Greek Dakota and flown back to Seoul, where a Firefly picked me up and flew me back to the ship to continue flying in 802."

'Pug' Mather was transferred to H.M.S GLORY later in the year at the end of OCEAN's first deployment. He was shot down once more on January 5th 1953 whilst on a bridge bombing mission, hit by a 76 mm shell, and became a prisoner of war until the end of hostilities. There were eventually four Royal Navy prisoners, the other three being Sub-Lieutenant D. Lankford RNVR, Pilot 3 R. H. Johnson and Naval Airman Penman. When 'Pug' Mather was repatriated he was welcomed back on board H.M.S OCEAN. An officer who was present described him as "a poor emaciated shrimp".

A tribute should be paid to the maintenance crews on board throughout the patrols. During the days of passage the aircraft were given their final checks. The flight deck machinery was brought up to scratch and the communications in the ship tested. The armourers had a full day preparing bombs and rockets so that by evening aircraft for the first detail on the following morning were all ready for launching. The last thing to be done before the ship steamed into the night was the spotting of the aircraft for the first detail, generally completed in the dog watches. Everyone took advantage of an early night in the knowledge that all had been done that could be done.

On July 27th the aircrews of OCEAN experienced a new development in the air war, when Russian built MiG XV jet fighters were seen further south than usual, in the Chinnampo area. Furys of 802 squadron, led by Lieutenant Hawkesworth engaged briefly with three MiG's, and as a result one Sea Fury was damaged and made a forced landing and the other three made their way back to the ship with superficial damage.

Sea Fury crash on deck 1952.

According to the pilots the Sea Fury was a dream to fly. Many people thought the plane was obsolete when the war in Korea broke out but it proved otherwise. None of the contemporary 'Jets' could match it's manoeuvrability. This was amply illustrated in the most famous encounter between the Sea Furys of 802 squadron and the Mig's, which came on August 9th, shortly after 6am, near Chinnampo. The flight consisted of Lieutenant Carmichael, Lieutenant Davis and Sub-Lieutenants Haines and Ellis. ' Hoagy' Carmichael later reported "We were reconnoitering in the area of a small village, Chinji-ri, north of Chinnampo. My number two, Sub-Lieutenant Carl Haines, called up unexpectedly "Mig's at five o'clock high, Mig's coming in". Eight Mig's came out of the sun. My number four, Sub-Lieutenant 'Smoo' Ellis gave a break when he noticed tracer streaming past his fuselage. Turning towards the MiG's we commenced a 'Scissors', conscious that four enemy planes were after each section of two Furys. By making our break turns we were able to present practically impossible targets. Pete Davis and 'Smoo' Ellis had good hits on one and he broke away. One MiG came head on and passed me. I saw his tracer shells and fired a burst. One sheered away, going north, out of range. I saw another MiG below me, going slowly; and I turned and fired - closing to 300 yards - firing all the time. Turning again I saw the aircraft crash and explode. For one terrible moment I thought it was one of my flight. I called 'Tell Off' and they all came back 'Two, Three, Four', and one of them said "Wizard a MiG. You've got him"."

Though Lieutenant Carmichael was credited with shooting down the first MiG, he always maintained that it was a team effort. The one that crashed had been fired on by all the members of the team. As Flight Leader he was given credit for the plane's destruction and awarded the D.S.C. on the recommendation of his C.O. Lieutenant Commander London, and the Captain, Charles Evans. To 'Hoagy' fell the honour of being the pilot of the only piston engined aircraft to shoot down a jet engined aircraft. Incidentally August 9th was Lieutenant Carmichael's birthday.

On July 10th /11th H.M.S OCEAN had been asked to provide two strikes, against the marshalling yards around Pyongyang, the North Korean capital. The city had been pounded by American aircraft for a considerable period. The yards were piled high with wooden crates thought to contain aircraft parts for MiG's. Twenty four sorties were made by 802 squadron Sea Fury's and 15 sorties by 825 squadron Firefly's. Many fires were started in the area, with no casualties to the two squadrons. The results were extremely satisfying. Admiral Scott-Moncrieff, accompanied by two American Admirals, witnessed the return of the second strike . He wrote "I was very pleased that Admiral Clark, an experienced airman, should see OCEAN operating. She did very well and our guests were suitably impressed". By the end of August, despite it's heavy defences, the battered city of Pyonyang had lost its military value for the rest of the war.

But it was not all work and no play. After each patrol OCEAN returned on alternate occasions to Kure or Sasebo for harbour replenishment. Both were able to provide the usual entertainment for sailors on shore leave. Wine, women and song were the order of the day. Sasebo, the UN base was described as a "haven of immorality with its girlie bars and massage parlours"; Kure, the Australian manned port, less so.
Kure was the first place to build supertankers, at the Ichikawajima shipyard, a base for the United Nations Naval Force. It was the ' home' for aircraft carriers and supply vessels on duty in the area , and also for the strong Australian contingent of destroyers, and at least two Canadian destroyers who acted as ' chasers' . From time to time troopships would enter port, their distinctive paintwork being white with a blue stripe and a beige funnel. Quite a busy harbour.

Nearby was an island used as a rest camp for the troops. Myajima Island was a rather large island in one of the inlets of the Inland Sea of Japan, about one hour's trip from Kure. The terrain was dominated by the fir-covered slopes of a mountain and on a strip of land between the foot of the mountain and the sea nestled the colourful little town of Itukusima; of great importance to the Shinto religion. Standing out in the harbour, directly facing a large Buddhist temple was a picturesque archway surmounted by a roof which looked like one storey of a pagoda. This was the sacred gateway to the Temple, painted a bright red it recalled childhood memories of a story book description of the Japanese way of life. During World War Two it was to this island that the Japanese suicide pilots, the Kamikazes, were sent to spend the last weeks of life in religious contemplation.

From the jetty those on leave walked a short distance to the hotel. The main building had been one of the finest in the vicinity and still retained the comfortable furnishings of earlier days. It was managed by three N.C.O's of the Australian Army and offered accommodation, sporting facilities, food and service second to none. Some guests climbed mountains, played vigorous games of tennis or relaxed in the slow movement of a slow boat. The small private beach was equipped with a diving raft - the water not too clean and contaminated by sullage, but even so was popular for swimming and, of course, there was always sunbathing. Evenings were occupied with drinking, watching films, or a quiet stroll around the town. The most popular venue was ' The Grotto' , a bar attached to the hotel. Unfortunately disaster struck, the hotel was razed to the ground and leave to this paradise suspended. OCEAN arrived back in Kure from the fifth patrol on August 1st and in the evening a concert was given on board featuring Bill Johnson, who had taken the role of Frank Butler opposite the Calamity Jane of Dolores Grey in the London production of ' Annie Get Your Gun' at the Coliseum. He was accompanied by his pianist and a comedian. In late September, again at Kure, the ships company welcomed another entertainer to their midst. Carole Carr was one of British radio's favourite singers of the day. Many men had written to her with requests for songs and messages for their families and themselves. She had almost 'adopted' the ship and frequently made reference to it in her broadcasts - and now she was in the area - visiting ships and land bases. On September 29th a helicopter from OCEAN picked her up from Iwakuni and she was brought to land on the crowded flight deck - all the ship's company waiting to see her in person, to welcome her and to have their photographs taken with her if possible. In the evening she was greeted by an ecstatic audience and presented with a bouquet by the youngest sailor on board. So she sang and joked with 'her' ship's company, all tightly packed into the hangar, some of the audience suspended from the most unlikely and dangerous viewpoints. She was always remembered with affection and later became an Honorary member of the H.M.S OCEAN Association until her death in January 1997.

An old Japanese cruiser, with the superstructure demolished, flattened, and filled in , formed a jetty which OCEAN, on her visits to Kure, would use. On one occasion it was the scene of a near disaster.

OCEAN was being refuelled with AVGAS, a very dangerous and highly flammable fuel, from on of the WAVE class RFA tankers. All bulkhead doors and scuttles were closed, and the pipe "No smoking throughout the ship" had been made - but only in English, because no-one thought to relay it in Japanese. Notices were also put up with the words "No Smoking and No Naked Flames" - in Chinese (probably because they were obtained in Hong Kong) but, again, not in Japanese. The Master-at-Arms had reported "Closed" to the Officer of the Day, and fuelling commenced. Suddenly, a gush of aviation fuel shot overboard into the sea between the ship and the fuel lighter. Within seconds it ignited, and the sea was ablaze and the burning fuel floated the length of the ship.

Before the fire-fighting party could tackle the blaze, flames began to creep up the paint on the port side of the ship, starting small fires on the quarter-deck in pockets of vapour that had accumulated. The flames continued to consume the paintwork on the ship's side and eventually reached the tail-planes of aircraft parked along the edge of the flight deck. . The pinnace, which had been sent ashore to collect mail, was approaching the gangway when it was surrounded by flames. The crew of four dived overboard to escape the holocaust, and the boat careered on it's own way to eventually coming to rest half a mile up river. The fires were prevented from spreading further and brought under control fairly quickly by the ship's well trained fire and emergency party with damage being restricted to the loss of seven aircraft, ammunition which had been thrown over the side at the height of the emergency, and smoke and heat damage to the paintwork. Amazingly, as the fire-fighting party fought to control the flames on the port side, libertymen fallen in on the jetty on the Starboard side were blissfully unaware of the emergency - as were other members of the ship's company taking their dinner in the messdecks.

So what had caused the fire? During the previous patrol, a bad landing by one of the aircraft had bent some fittings on the port side, including a gun sponson. Japanese welders had been brought onboard to repair the damage, but had been dismissed for the day while the fuelling was taking place. However, one welder was unaware of the warning given, and continued to work on the catapult sponson. A burning piece of metal had fallen into the sea and ignited the fuel which had drifted along from the original spillage. No one knows what happened to him - he never reported back to work in the dockyard, and no sign of his body was ever found.

On October 13th, on the last day of the ninth patrol, the First Sea Lord, Admiral Sir Roderic McGrigor paid a visit to OCEAN, accompanied by Rear Admiral Clifford (FO2FES) and Admiral Sir Guy Russell. They were transferred by jackstay from H.M.S BIRMINGHAM for a three hour visit. Later, on November 1st at the end of the final patrol, there was another visit by Rear Admiral Clifford. He gave a short speech of appreciation to the assembled ship's company -"OCEAN's record in Korean waters is outstanding and is an example of what can be achieved by bold leadership and good teamwork. The spirit, courage and skill of her well led squadrons have resulted in much damage to the enemy and have been backed up by the consistently high standard of the conduct and tempo of her maintenance deck operations." Tuesday October 30th had been the last day of the last patrol, Firefly 282 piloted by Mr Wigg circled and landed on OCEAN's deck, thus ending the ship's tour of duty.

Later on the same day a short service was held in memory of the eight shipmates who had lost their lives during the campaign. Members of the ship's company gathered on the after end of the flight deck, under the half-masted Ensign. Prayers were said, and after the bugler sounded the last post, wreaths were cast overboard to float away in the gathering darkness. It was finally time for the ship to return to Malta.

On her homeward journey OCEAN reached Hong Kong on November 5th and joined H.M.S GLORY, her relief ship, in a large scale mock war exercise call Tai Pan, to test the defences of Hong Kong itself. Six days later, at Singapore, OCEAN met up with H.M.S UNICORN, the maintenance aircraft carrier which throughout the whole Korean campaign had worked to keep the operational carriers supplied with aircraft, spares and essential supplies. OCEAN transferred aircraft to be used by other squadrons and on the 13th sailed for the Red Sea and on the 25th reached Port Suez, where she anchored and joined company with a line of merchantmen waiting to transit the Canal. On the 26th a farewell concert was given on board in the hangar, the ' Polio Sisters' making a welcome return visit for one more performance, the ginger moustache still very much in evidence on the tallest 'lady'. A first rate show by all performers, including the resident Royal Marine's Band.

In January 1953 H.M.S OCEAN and her squadrons were awarded the Boyd Trophy in recognition of outstanding service in the Korean War.

Flying statistics for OCEAN's first tour of duty in Korean Waters

Total Korean Sorties 5945

Record daily sorties 123

Record number of sorties in one patrol 767

Sortie rate per day 76.3

 Total rocket projectiles16, 490

Total 500lb bombs used 3, 454

Total 1000lb bombs used420

Total deck landings since commissioning 9, 273

Total deck landings 802 and 825 squadrons7, 160

Best average Sea Fury landing interval 17 secs

Best average Sea Fury catapult launch interval 33.7 secs

Best average Firefly landing interval 19 secs

Best average Firefly catapult launch interval36 secs

Number of incident free deck landings1, 613

Deck landing accident rate 1 per 398

Under way for Korea. April 5th 1952. Malta

Loading bombs prior to deployment. To Korea, Malta 1952. Crown Copyright.

HMS Ocean leaving Grand Harbour for Korea. 1952.

Aden 1952

Suez Canal

The ships main generator. Steel bands became unsoldered and ripped the ends of the armature and field coils

Executing a Pin-Wheel Grand Harbour. Valetta 1952.

Sasebo 1952

Forces Rest hotel Miya Jima 1952.

Shinto Shrine Miya Jima 1952.

The Chopper lands. Westland Sikorsky S51 Dragon Fly. Hong Kong 1952.

Bomb loading and more ammo for a Firefly. Korea 1952.

Fitting 1000 lb bombs. Korea.

Fireflies fitted with rockets Korea.

HMS Ocean berthed in Kure with Empire Hallindale. HMS Unicorn in the background.

Aircraft being stowed forward. Korea.

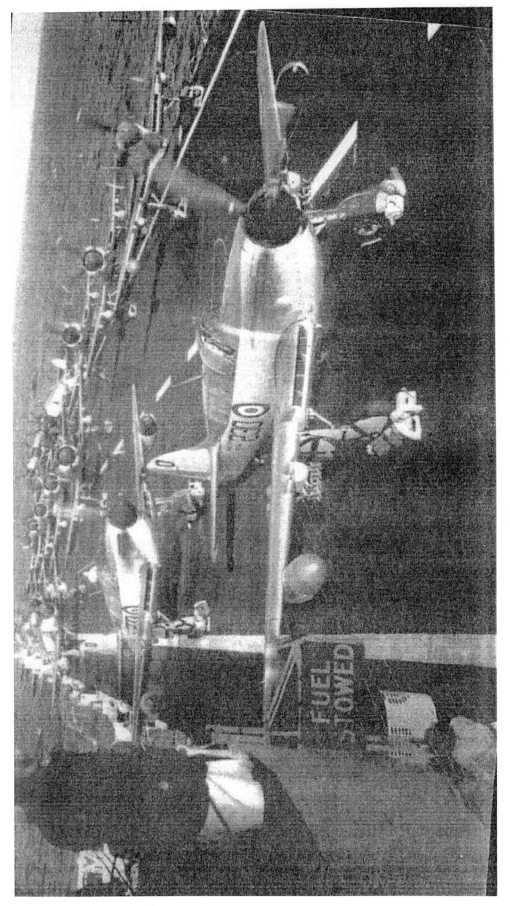

Preparing for take-off in Korean waters 1952.

Bomb runs and Chinnampo Bridge. Korea 1952

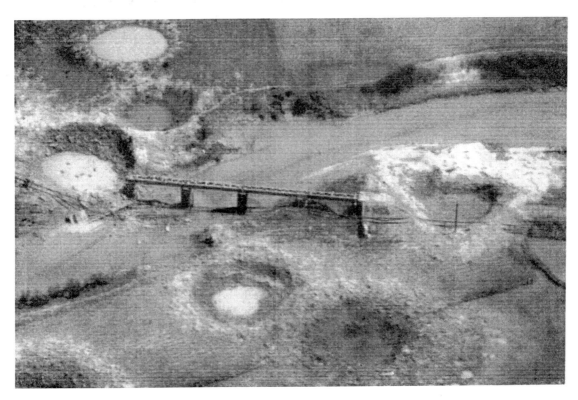

On passage to Korea 1952. Crown Copyright.

Commander "Hoagy" Carmichael with flight crew. Korea 1952

"Hoagy" spinning a yarn. Korea 1952

Peter "Hoagy" Carmichael 1952.

Viscount Alexander pays a visit to HMS Ocean. Korea 1952. Crown Copyright.

The First Sea Lord, Admiral Sir Roderic McGrigor pays a visit to HMS Ocean. Korea 1952. Crown Copyright.

The youngest member of the ship's company makes a presentation to Carole Carr. 1952

Captain Crash Evans welcomes Carole Carr. 1952. Crown Copyright

The famous "Polio Sisters" rise again. 1952

TEZUKA MASSAGE HOSPITAL

Please lay 'down and have yourself A Massage here so that you will be able to recover from your fatigue, which you have received from the battle fields. We always have very beautiful massage girls to welcome you Soldiers And Sailors and Seaman. Sanitary Conditions Hepting System is Perfect!

(From A.M.10 To P.M.9)

TEZUKA MASSAGE HOSPITAL
5-3, SIMANJI-CHO

Any volunteers ?

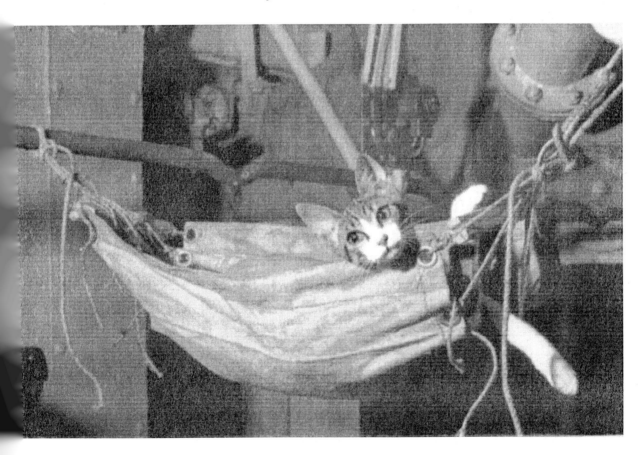

All the comforts of home.

Return to Malta and Return to Korea

And so back to the Mediterranean past the island of Crete. On November 28th, within the sight of the breakwater of Grand Harbour, a salute was fired in welcome and a flight of Fireflies from H.M.S THESEUS passed overhead in a greeting to the ship now back in peaceful waters. On Sunday November 30th Divisions were inspected by HRH The Duke of Edinburgh accompanied by the Earl Mountbatten of Burma. Other ships in harbour sent their contingents to parade on OCEAN's flight deck for the ceremony. Two days later the Captain, Charles Evans made his final appearance on board, when he relinquished his command to Captain B.E.W (Lofty) Logan who had already been in command of the ship during the trooping period in 1950. 'Crash' Evans left the ship in traditional fashion, in a whaler manned by senior officers; to the cheers of a ship's company who had a great affection and respect for their Captain of the Korean period. The following Sunday divisions were attended by the C-in-C and F.O. (Air) Mediterranean Fleet.

On January 1st 1953, 898 squadron was officially disbanded and officers and men absorbed into 807 squadron Sea Furies under the command of Lieutenant Commander T.L.M. Brander. 810 squadron was commanded by Lieutenant Commander A.W. (Pants) Bloomer. They were to be the two squadrons on board for the second tour of Korea and until the ship returned to the United Kingdom in December 1953.

On New Years Day 1953 the ship left Malta for a cruise to Crete, where she was to take part in an exercise with the Greek Army and 42 Royal Marine Commando. She reached Suda Bay on the 3rd and was visited by the Governor General of the island. During the exercise the ship's aircraft provided air cover when 42 Commando and the ship's own Royal Marine Detachment fought a mock battle against the Greek Army.

Returning to Malta on January 15th, with the squadrons flown off to Hal Far, OCEAN went into dry dock until March 19th. However, on February 6th, although still in dry dock, the ship was dressed overall on the occasion of the first anniversary of the accession of Her Majesty Queen Elizabeth to the throne.

Out of dry dock and looking trim, a children's party was held in the hangar on April 4th. A most happy occasion, although by now the ship's company already knew that soon they would be heading out once more for the Korean war. There had been some indication that OCEAN would return to the Far East

HRH The Duke of Edinburgh, accompanied by Earl Mountbatten, inspects the Ship's company. Malta 1952. Crown Copyright.

HRH The Duke of Edinburgh, accompanied by Earl Mountbatten, inspects the Ship's company. Malta 1952. Crown Copyright.

Admiral Lord Loius Mountbatten inspects divisions. Grand Harbour. Malta 1953. Crown Copyright

Captain Charles Evans. Relinquishes his command. Malta 1952.

Engineering Team. Sasebo 1953.

Back row. S/Lt Shaw, S/Lt Daw, Lt Sherriff

Middle row. S/Lt Robinson, Mr Thaxter, S/Lt Bage, Mr Bruty, Mr Maltby

Front row. Lt Maclean, CDR Tucker, Lt CDR Harcus, Lt O'Hara

and the exercises in Crete had been an ideal training ground for the squadrons because the local terrain was similar to that in Korea.

OCEAN sailed for the war area once more on April 16th 1953. The Earl Mountbatten of Burma had visited the ship and after inspecting Divisions bid her men farewell in a very stirring and at times amusing speech. An Armistice in Korea had been strongly reported, but it was still necessary for the ship to take over the East coast operations from H.M.S GLORY which had been on duty since the previous November. However negotiations were at a stalemate. There had been much discussion and just as much disagreement. The Chinese steadfastly demanded that all foreign troops be withdrawn from Korea, and the United Nations equally steadfastly refused. Another issue was one of boundaries. The Communists demanded that the 38th Parallel be restored, the United States insisting on the existing battle line. The most important issue - the U. N. forces held 171, 000 prisoners, 50, 000 of who were unwilling to return to a Communist country. The Communists wanted all the prisoners back. The negotiations deadlock did not resume until after the death of Stalin. In April the first 6, 670 Communists and the 684 U. N. prisoners were exchanged at Panmunjon. Syngman Rhee was opposed to terms that would divide Korea and demanded that the offensive was resumed.

OCEAN retraced her steps to the Far East once more and on Sunday May 17th sailed into Sasebo harbour, renewing her acquaintance with H.M.S GLORY and transferring her serviceable aircraft before her departure for England now that she had finished her tour. The final signal was sent by OCEAN to the departing ship. "*Ecclesiastes Chapter Nine, Verse Seven*" which translates "*Go they way, eat thy bread with joy, and drink thy wine with a merry heart, for God now accepteth thy works*"

Once more the ship's work began, the general pattern being the same as for the first tour in 1952. Five patrols in all before her own departure from the scene. Targeting of rail and road bridges, strafing troops, reconnaissance and air spot on enemy gun positions. On May 25th Vice Admiral Clark in flag ship U.S.S. NEW JERSEY, accompanied by Rear Admiral Clifford in H.M..S NEWCASTLE met and called on President Syngman Rhee in Seoul. Later on the same day a large blue helicopter called 'Jersey Bump' arrived on board OCEAN with Vice Admiral Clark and Rear Admiral Clifford. After the Admirals had observed a flight programme, the helicopter returned to transfer them to their respective ships. On May 30th, at the end of the first patrol, Admiral Clifford transferred his Flag to OCEAN to passage to Sasebo.

On May 31st at 16.30 fourteen Sea Furies of 807 squadron disembarked from OCEAN's flight deck for a flypast over the Commonwealth Divisions in celebration of the Coronation of Queen Elizabeth the Second. The carrier was moored at her buoy in the harbour after her return from the first patrol. There was no cross wind across her deck and a tug swung her round pointing in a safe direction away from the hills and other ships in harbour. RATOG was used , a feat unprecedented in Fleet Air Arm history and one which became the talk of the United Nations Fleet for days, enhancing even further the already high the reputation of the British pilots. After forming up the Furies passed over the ship in formation of 'E. R.' on their way to Iwakuni. On landing there they unfortunately had to park the aircraft overnight on open ground in a night of pouring rain. The following day it was found that two aircraft were unserviceable, their radios out of action, and others reluctant to start their engines. The rest headed for Seoul and the display area and were able to arrange a recognisable 'E' but no 'R' at all.

On June 2nd (Coronation Day) all eyes were focused on the British ships, H.M.S OCEAN and H.M.S TYNE, the depot ship, and the several Commonwealth and Netherland ships in the harbour. They, together with ships of other nations, were dressed overall. In the hangar H.M.S OCEAN played host to representatives from many ships - The Flag Office Second in Command Far East, Rear Admiral E.G.A. Clifford. The Commander 7th Fleet Vice Admiral J.J. Clark, U.S.N. , the Commander Task Force 95 Rear Admiral C. E. Olsen and the Governor of Nagasaki.

It had been planned to use OCEAN's flight deck for the ceremony, but a last minute downpour prevented it and a simple service and parade was held in the hangar; culminating in 'Three cheers for her Majesty' and the welcome order 'Splice the Mainbrace'. Even the Chinese stewards were allowed a 'TOT' for the occasion on special dispensation by the Flag Captain and Admiral which had been put forward as a request by OCEAN's captain B.E.W. Logan. Lunch for the principal guests was given by Admiral Clifford on board TYNE and the remainder on OCEAN. In the evening there was searchlight display by all ships and a reception given for 200 guests on board. Great interest was shown by the American servicemen and broadcasts and news from England were relayed by the American Forces Radio Service. There was also Japanese interest in the event. Banners showing the Royal crown appeared in the main

Pete Shephard   Bill Whant

Left to Right. Dave Bawden, Bob Breakspear, Hayes, Terry Martin, Colin Hick, Bob Pearson, Leeson, Jan Mulder, Harry Hanes, Van Cougton, Ivan Brown, Halliday, George Duce, Laurie Brander, Gus Hagborn, Dave Hiln, Mitchell, Cross, Jasper Crawford, Bill Ayrs, Norman Wood, Don Pugh, Ted Anson

807 Squadron Officers Group. 1952

streets. On the following day two marquees were set up in a large town square with a bar serving drinks and snacks free to the U. N. forces, courtesy of the local Chamber of Commerce. There were celebrations to a lesser extent in Kure and Tokyo. All ships in the war area were dressed with masthead flags.

Celebrations over, work again came to the fore as OCEAN embarked for the second patrol. The main task was to effect a blockade to ensure that the North Koreans did not bring up supplies by sea or dislodge the United nations land forces from the islands off the coast. To affect the enemy communications, supplies, troops, billets and support the U. N. ships in the area. OCEAN embarked on the second patrol on June 8th to relieve the U.S.S BAIROKO. This day also saw the signing of the prisoner of war agreement, bringing the Armistice much nearer.

During the third patrol the weather closed in again at times, making the operations difficult, but by the time the ship reached Sasebo, on July 7th after a rough passage, 474 sorties had been flown, an average of 86 per day when flying was possible.

On June 18th Rhee released 27, 000 North Korean anti-Communist prisoners in defiance of the U. N., and the Communists broke off relations. However, on July 20th, after much haggling with the United States over economic aid, a security pact to protect South Korea from further aggression was reached. Rhee agreed and the Armistice was finally signed on July 27th. A Neutral Nations Commission for Repatriation started the repatriation of prisoners. There were 21, 809, of whom 7, 82 Korean and 14, 227 Chinese chose to stay in South Korea or Taiwan. Economic reparations were made on assistance programs together with U. N. emergency relief.

OCEAN had sailed for the fourth patrol on July 14th and experienced fog, rain and low cloud conditions. Some sorties were curtailed and some aircraft had to be directed to their targets by RADAR. On one occasion the fog was so dense that Sea Furies had to be diverted to K16 (Kimpo) airfield. On the next day July 15th , the catapult became unserviceable and the Fireflies and Sea Furies for the next mission were launched by RATOG. One Firefly crashed with the loss of life of both members of the crew. The pilot Lieutenant A.J. Evans was rescued but died later. The body of Lieutenant K.M. Thomas was never recovered. On the same day a burial service was held for both men on the after end of the flight deck, when the Pilot's body was committed to the deep and the Observer was remembered in the prayers of those who attended.

On July 16th, three Fireflies disembarked for K14 airfield (Pyontaek), for use as nightfighters, operating with Aircraft Control and Warning Squadron, United States Air Force located on a hill north of Seoul. This was in response to the night time incursions by very ancient small enemy bi-planes (PO2's) - the 'bed check Charlies' on nuisance missions, After a while YAK 9's were used in their place, their low speed and manoeuvrability allowing them to operate out of tiny strips in mountainous country - some of it within the Panmunjom Truce Zone. The cry had gone out for some slow Allied aircraft, and Captain Logan's contribution was the three Fireflies of 810 squadron, led by Lieutenant Commander 'Pants' Bloomer together with seven officers and sixteen ratings, with Lieutenant C. A. Spensley as Night Fighter Direction officer. During the short time up to the signing of the truce 810 detachment flew 64 hours 35 minutes, a total of 31 missions. After the Truce was signed the aircraft immediately switched to police duties - patrolling the demarcation line throughout the night to prevent any violation of the demilitarised zone by any aircraft. On August 9th the detachment, having been the first Commonwealth night fighters of the Korean War, returned to OCEAN, their duties at an end, . Captain Logan wrote 'The success of this venture, laid on a short notice and with little material backing, reflects great credit on the aircrew concerned and in particular Lieutenant Commander Bloomer, Commanding officer, 810 squadron, who carried out all the initial flying tests and inspired the who unit with enthusiasm by his own personal example.

On the signing of the Armistice, OCEAN became involved in the operation to evacuate islands occupied north of a line running south west of the Han estuary including Chodo and Sok-to. The Armistice terms required them to be evacuated within five days of the signatures. OCEAN's role was to cover the withdrawals and assist in silencing shore batteries with 807 Sea Fury bombing raids. 810 squadron Fireflies concentrated on rocket raids. Bad weather dogged these operations, but by the end of the patrol and the ship's return to Kure 539 sorties had been flown. During these bomb attacks Lieutenant Hands made the 1000th deck landing of 807 Sea Furies since the squadron left Hal Far at the beginning of 1953.

On strafing runs low flying presented many hazards and aircraft returned to base well peppered - a hole in the engine, a hole half and an inch from the fuel feed. Others with holes in the rear cockpit, wings

THE ORDER OF PARADE

and

FORM OF SERVICE

in

H.M.S. OCEAN

———————

IN HONOUR OF THE

CORONATION

OF HER MAJESTY

QUEEN ELIZABETH II

Tuesday, 2nd June, 1953

Order of Parade

1110	The Flag Officer, Second-in-Command, Far East Station, Rear-Admiral E. G. A. Clifford, C.B., arrives H.M.S. Ocean.
1115	The Governor of Nagasaki Prefecture arrives H.M.S. Ocean.
1118	The Commander Task Force 95, Rear-Admiral C. E. Olsen, United States Navy, arrives H.M.S. Ocean.
1120	The Commander United States Seventh Fleet, Vice-Admiral J. J. Clark, United States Navy, arrives H.M.S. Ocean.
1125	Rear-Admiral E. G. A. Clifford, accompanied by Vice-Admiral J. J. Clark and Rear-Admiral C. E. Olsen, received by Royal Marine Guard furnished by H.M.S. Ocean on the Flight Deck.
1130-1140	The Parade inspected by Rear-Admiral E. G. A. Clifford, accompanied by Vice-Admiral J. J. Clark and Rear-Admiral C. E. Olsen.
1140	The Parade closed for Divine Service.
1200	ROYAL SALUTE OF TWENTY ONE GUNS. On completion of the Royal Salute, the Parade will sing the National Anthem accompanied by the Band.
1205	Three Cheers for Her Majesty Queen Elizabeth, called by the Flag Officer, Second-in-Command, Far East Station.
1210	The Flag Officer, Second-in-Command, Far East Station leaves H.M.S. Ocean.
1215	Guests attending the luncheon given by the Flag Officer, Second-in-Command, Far East Station, leave H.M.S. Ocean.

Note: Guests are requested to be onboard H.M.S. Ocean by 1100

Coronation Order of Parade

and tails and some pilots had to ditch their aircraft in the sea - but there were no fatalities. Commander Harper remembers that on one occasion Lieutenant Bacon ditched his aircraft over the sea and was promptly picked up by a U. S. rescue helicopter. We sent a signal to the Yanks 'Thank you for saving our Bacon' and also a bottle of whisky for the pilot (which is apparently an old OCEAN custom). The next day a Sea Fury pilot Lieutenant Hicks had to ditch with engine failure. His aircraft sank very quickly and luckily he was plucked from the sea pretty quickly by the U. S. helicopter from Paengyongdo. For this escape a second bottle of whisky was sent with the message 'Thanks for the Hick-up' There was bad weather on most days, but by the end of this patrol and the ship's return to Kure, 539 sorties had been flown.

Landings and takeoffs could also be very hazardous, particularly in very foggy weather. Sub Lieutenant Sheppard, who ran short of fuel had to make an emergency landing. Owing to the dense fog he couldn't see the ship and had to be talked down to the flight deck. His Sea Fury suddenly appeared to land and veer off, missing the bridge by very little, but landing safely. On another occasion the catapult broke down and the Commander (Air) decided to send the next detail off by RATOG. The first Sea Fury went off all right but the second fired his rockets too soon and he went straight over the bows into the sea, where his aircraft quickly disintegrated. He was swiftly picked up by Lieutenant Earl in the ship's helicopter. Every take off and landing on a carrier was fraught with danger, but it was quite astonishing what the pilots seemed to get away with. There were two helicopter pilots on board, very different characters. Lieutenant Earl - mercurial - throwing his helicopter about with seeming wild abandon, descending to the crest of the waves and sliding about in sweeping turns - nevertheless an expert pilot; and Lieutenant Hooker, a New Zealander - safe and steady - but both men invaluable in a crisis.

Representatives of many nations gather to celebrate the Coronation Day Parade and Service in the hanger on board HMS Ocean.

Guard provided by Royal marines of the ship's detachment. Coronation Day on board HMS Ocean. Crown Copyright.

FO2 calls for "Three Cheers"

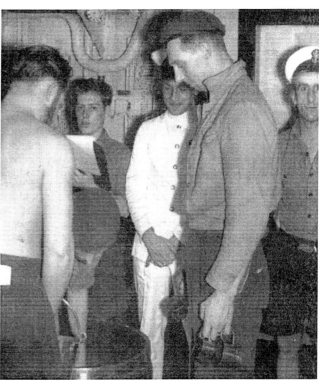

"Splice the Main Brace"

R.A.T.O.G. take off for Coronation fly past. HMS Ocean is tied up to the buoy. Sasebo.

Captain B.E.W. "Lofty" Logan takes command. Malta 1952.

Chapel of St Peter. HMS Ocean.

Funeral service on board for Lt(P) Evans and Lt (O) Thomas. July 1953.

Nakadori, Kure 1953

"Slipstream show with RM Band. 1953

American helicop-ters on board. 1953

Party given for members of the Ship's Company by a shipbuilding company. Kure 1953

Open day Yokohama 1953.

Throughout the months of August and September OCEAN kept up her patrols. She was there on the spot, in case of any violation of the truce and to keep her crew ready for action if need be. But, in general, life was easier. The Korean War had been quite unlike the action in World War Two, in which many of her crew had take part, where times of intensive action would be followed by a lull of mere watchfulness. But in Korea, the target was always there, there was no lull and whilst on patrol for nine days at a time, it was a daily round of landing and taking off, maintenance, ammunition loading and the matters of daily life. Until the ship reached harbour once more there was no let up.

OCEAN sailed for her fifth patrol on Friday July 31st at 4.00pm. On Saturday morning at 5.30am the ships company woke to a heavy pounding and the ship going astern. The ship was grounded momentarily in the Shmononeki Strait - the condenser inlets were jammed with coral fragments and after struggling through the strait the ship had to anchor until the inlets could be cleared. Later, exercises were carried out with H.M.S UNICORN, when some of the Sea Furies flew on to exercise all their ground crews and to give OCEAN's airmen a look at a different flight deck for a change. A more peaceful patrol than of late. OCEAN sailed for four more patrols before heading back for Great Britain, but there was no return to hostilities - the final patrol being from the 12th to the 16th October.

The programme of the last few weeks of the commission in the area was announced, and instead of the usual calls to Sasebo and Kure, Yokohama (the principal port of Japan) was to be the next port of call.

On the day before the arrival at Yokohama it had been Harvest Festival in the little chapel of St Peter on board the ship. The chapel was decorated traditionally with sheaves of corn and bread in many shapes, baked in OCEAN's own bakery, together with flowers and fruits of the harvest. Since the ship had first commissioned in 1945 the chapel had served it's purpose on may occasions, a haven from the noisy and warlike atmosphere of the rest of the ship for many of the ships company, with services of may denominations from time to time.

Throughout the following nine days there were leave parties to the British Commonwealth camp at Ebisu near Tokyo and the American Rest and Recuperation Centre in Yokohama. Many men had a well earned three days rest and some took day trips to Tokyo and other places of interest. For two days in that period certain parts of the ship were thrown open to the Japanese. People - thousands of people. The crash barriers on the docks were swept away like matchwood, the dockside had to be seen to be believed, but all the visitors were apparently most impressed with what they saw. On another day there was a children's party with some of the crew dressed as pirates for the occasion. One day members of the ships company paid a visit to Hiroshima, the most thought provoking scene of the Atomic bomb. An officer in charge remembers an incident involving one of the ships company. There was already at this time a sprinkling of tourists to the ruins of the city, mostly Americans. Among the 'attractions' of the day were survivors of the bomb showing their injuries and begging for money. OCEAN had on board a hardened veteran stoker, badly burned and scarred years before on another ship in the boiler room. As enterprising as ever he proceeded to discard his shirt and went around the sightseers cap in hand, and was surprisingly successful in gaining a little extra beer money.

On Wednesday September 30th OCEAN sailed for her long last patrol. Having said her farewells to Sasebo and Kure and with the coming of H.M.A.S SYDNEY to take over her duties, OCEAN's tour was at an end and she sailed for home. She had earned another battle honour - Korea 1952 - 53

TO THE MEMORY OF THE MEN WHO LOST THEIR LIVES DURING THE KOREAN CAMPAIGN.

Kenneth Macdonald Lieutenant (E) (P)14th May 1952
Timothy J. C. Williamson -Napier Lieutenant Commander (P)19th May 1952
Leslie M. Edwards Aircrewman (1)19th May 1952
Richard F. Herbert Naval Airman (1) 19th May 1952
Alan Findlay S.B.A 4th June 1952
Robert C. Hunter Lieutenant (P) 4th July 1952
Donald A. Dick Lieutenant Commander24th July 1952
Kenneth P. Jordan Radio Elect (Air)29th July 1952
James Millar Naval Airman (1)11th May 1953
Albert J. D. Evans Lieutenant (P)15th July 1953
Kenneth Maxwell Thomas Lieutenant (O)15th July 1953

Training, Trogs and Musketeer

On December 17th 1953 H.M.S OCEAN arrived in Plymouth Sound - home at last after 2 ½ years service in foreign waters during which time the ship had travelled a total of 131, 650 miles.   Among other statistics - £56, 000 had been paid to officers and men in hard earned wages, £17, 000 of withdrawals had been repaid to 2, 200 intrepid ' rabbit hunters' and 90, 000, 000 Japanese Yen and other currencies were exchanged during the tours to the Far East.   90, 000 yard of electric cable, 78 arrester hooks for aircraft, 5, 000 aircraft propeller washers and 100 sets of aircraft drop tanks had been issued; together with the mundane day to day requirements of 1, 709, 125 lbs of potatoes, 200, 000 lbs of beef, 46, 000 lbs of sausages, 18, 000 tins of fruit - and a rum ration of 80, 000 pints in 520 barrels.

Many noteworthy events had occurred at home during the ships absence.   Identity cards were abolished in 1952; in May of the same year the first scheduled passenger jet flight took place with a Comet, from London to Johannesburg; and King Farouk abdicated the throne in Egypt (an event eventually leading to the crisis at Suez in 1956).   It was not until February 1953 that sweet rationing finished after World War Two, in March of that year Stalin died and in April the Royal Yacht BRITANNIA was launched. The Coronation of Her Majesty Queen Elizabeth had taken place on June 2nd preceded by the announcement on May 29th that Mount Everest had been conquered by Hillary, Hunt and the Sherpa Tensing.

Captain Logan relinquished his command of the ship in late January 1954 and on 24th February H.M.S OCEAN moved to no 10 dry dock for a refit as a training vessel with the Home Fleet Training Squadron based at Portland.   The hangar deck was partly taken up with messes for the ' trogs' , as the ship's company came to call the trainees.   On the port side of the hangar, just aft of midships, was a large structure used as a store-room and surmounted by a mock bridge, complete with binnacles, etc., for training purposes.   The hangar was used as a gym, parade ground in wet weather, and as a garage for the cranes used to move the boats from the flight deck.   The flight deck itself was ringed with boats on trolleys, and there was a rectangular structure abaft the after lift.   Divisions were held on the flight deck, but it was also used for deck-hockey and other sports.   It was surprisingly uneven - reputedly a legacy from the first deck landings by jet aircraft.

At the end of World War Two it was decided that conscription of servicemen should continue, and under the National Service Acts of 1947-48 every male citizen between the ages of 18 and 26 years was liable for 18 months compulsory service with 4 years on the reserve.   In 1950 this was amended to 2 years actual service with 3¼ years on the reserve - and from mid 1954 until the end of the ship's life in 1957 OCEAN was to train quite a number of them.

By the beginning of June 1954 the ship was out of dry dock and ready to resume service.   Captain H. C. Browne assumed command on August 9th, and after Navy Days in Portland in September the ship weighed for Gibraltar for exercises, calling at Tangier on her return journey at the end of November.

In late January 1955 and again in early March OCEAN proceeded for further exercises with H.M.S THESEUS (known universally as Tea Issue), first to Brest and then to Gibraltar.   On April 4th Captain E. G. Roper took over command of the ship from Captain Browne and in late May the ship embarked for exercises and visits in northern waters; firstly to Liverpool and then to Greenock, Tail of the Bank and Lock Eriboll.

One officer remembers that the navy had always been particularly welcome in Liverpool, the home port of Captain Johnnie Walker and his men, the scourge of the U Boats in World War Two and the heroes of the Battle of the Atlantic.   OCEAN's company were welcomed to Bootle and could do no wrong.   On the Saturday night a dance was held for the sailors at Liverpool Town Hall.   All the nice girls love a sailor and the evening was no exception.   But all the girls had local boyfriends - Teddy Boys.   That evening an army of them were waiting outside at the end of the dance for a great punch up.   OCEAN'S Jolly Jacks sorted them out, with police standing at the back, just watching.   The following day a senior police officer was heard to say "Could you come back again? We have had a lot of trouble with these lads recently".

At the end of June OCEAN proceeded to Hamburg for a courtesy visit and berthed alongside Uberseebrucke for five days with the ship open to visitors on 1st/2nd July; and then, heading south on her return journey, called into Margate and anchored in the thick fog - an eerie experience when only the mast of neighbouring ships were visible form the flight deck on board the carrier. From mid September the ship embarked for Malta on two occasions carrying troops and stores to Cyprus and making calls at Port Said and Tangier on the return journeys; finally arriving back in Portland on December 1st an in time for Christmas leave.

In the last eighteen months OCEAN's cap ribbon had been seen from the highest rocks of Eriboll, to Hamburg and as far as the smelliest wharves of Famagusta. Not bad for a training ship which was popularly supposed to spend it's life swinging round the buoy in Portland and grounding on piles of empty tins.

In early January 1956 OCEAN left Portland for exercises in Arosa Bay, Vigo, and on her return to Devonport at the end of the same month went into dry dock to refit to give her the capability of operating helicopters. Back in service in June the ship sailed once more for Hamburg, calling on West Hartlepool on her return journey. The first of the year's trooping was made in August when 1, 334 officers, men of the 21st and 50th Medium Regiments Royal Artillery with transport were embarked for Famagusta. After a quick turn round the ship returned to Malta with 864 officers and men of 40 Royal Marine Commando, and then returned to the UK by the end of the month. On September 12th Captain I.W.T.. Beloe assumed command from Captain E. G. Roper and then a period of exercises followed off Spithead with the Joint Helicopter Unit on board, and in the company of H.M.S THESEUS carrying 845 squadron.

In July 1952 the fun loving , corrupt King Farouk of Egypt had abdicated the throne in favour of his infant son, and in June 1953 the young king was deposed by General Mohammed Neguib. He , in turn, was to be replaced by Lieutenant Colonel Gamel Abdel Nasser, the Prime Minister, in a classic coup, orchestrated by the Revolutionary Council of which he was head. Anti Western and hostile to Israel, he initiated the take over and nationalisation for the Suez Canal on July 26th 1956; when tension arose from the withdrawal of Anglo-American funds for the Aswan Dam. Egypt's only major source of revenue was the Suez Canal and in response the Egyptian government seized all revenues; although the Canal was still owned jointly by France and Britain. The British Government were persuaded by the United States to lay the case before U. N. arbitration , but by October the talks were stalemate and Anthony Eden together with the French Premier Mollet were losing patience. On October 29th Israel dropped paratroopers at the eastern end of Mitla Pass, the gateway to Sinai, thus invading the Egyptian border and putting Operation Kadesh into action.

On the same day three British carriers slipped from Malta with their escorts, steaming east at high speed. From the beginning of November RAF Canberras and Valiants from Malta and Cyprus, together with Sea Hawks and Sea Venoms from the carriers made strikes on airfields in the Nile Delta; hoping to destroy the Egyptian Air Force potential.

On October 27th OCEAN had received orders to proceed to Malta at full speed carrying 145 members of JEHU and their 12 aircraft and 56 vehicles. On her arrival the ship embarked part of 45 Commando, 215 Wing RAF and 9 Movement Control. On November 3rd the ship sailed for Port Said and ' Operation Musketeer' , Sir Manley Power flying his flag in H.M.S EAGLE. The fleet also included OCEAN's sister ship H.M.S THESEUS. OCEAN carried Whirlwinds and Sycamores of the Joint (Army and RAF) Experimental Helicopter Unit and THESEUS the Whirlwinds of 845 Squadron.

The assault proper came on November 5th when the Third Battalion Parachute Regiment dropped on the airfield at El Gamil and French Paratroopers dropped on Port Fuad. During these initial operations two fleets were converging on a rendezvous 30 miles north of Port Said, from Malta and Cyprus. At the same time the French were operating on the eastern side of the entrance to the Canal off Port Fouad.

Early on November 6th landing craft of the Amphibious Warfare Squadron transported 40 and 42 Commandos to the beaches. OCEAN anchored in the swept channel about 8 miles from the shore and as soon as the beach head was secured the call came for the 45 Commando Unit to be landed as initial reinforcements.

The first flight was off just after 7 am on November 6th, and the operation went smoothly except for an accident to leading Sycamore; but fortunately there were no casualties. Within 70 minutes all troops were on shore, and the joint helicopters had made 193 sorties. A historic day - the combined efforts of the airlift of men and stores from H.M.S OCEAN and H.M.S THESEUS saw the first helicopter - borne

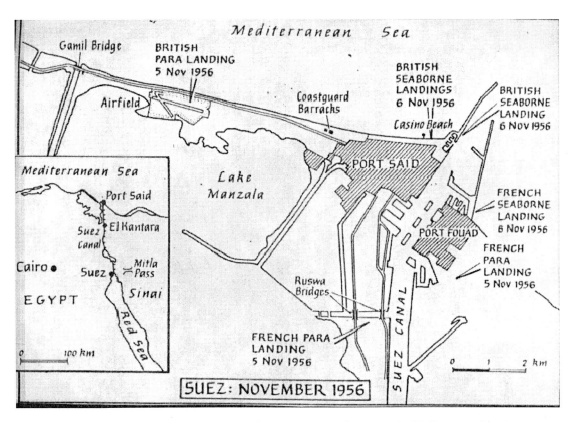

Mediterranean Sea

Gamil Bridge

BRITISH PARA LANDING 5 Nov 1956

Airfield

Coastguard Barracks

BRITISH SEABORNE LANDINGS 6 Nov 1956

BRITISH SEABORNE LANDING 6 NOV 1956

Casino Beach

Lake Manzala

PORT SAID

FRENCH SEABORNE LANDING 6 Nov 1956

PORT FOUAD

FRENCH PARA LANDING 5 Nov 1956

Ruswa Bridges

SUEZ CANAL

FRENCH PARA LANDING 5 Nov 1956

Mediterranean Sea

Port Said

El Kantara

Suez Canal

Cairo

Suez

Mitla Pass

EGYPT

Sinai

Red Sea

0   100 km

0   1   2 km

SUEZ: NOVEMBER 1956

assault landing in British Naval History and the creation of Commando Helicopter Carriers for future operations.

OCEAN had embarked extra medical stores and the regular medical staff had been augmented by two specialist medical officers, together with 10 sick bay attendants staff from the Royal Naval Hospital Plymouth. The ship's library had been converted to provide an additional operating the theatre, and part of the hangar had been modified to provide additional sick-berth accommodation. Once the landings were completed the helicopters started to evacuate the wounded on their return journeys and at the end of the day a total of 39 casualties had been received on board including 4 Egyptians (two of whom were under 15 year of age). These were returned ashore after treatment. During the three days following the landings 32 surgical operations were performed on board by Surgeon Lieutenant Commander Etherington and his team. Many men suffered serious injuries, but not one treated on OCEAN died.

In the late afternoon of 6th November OCEAN moved into the harbour, mooring just ahead of the French Hospital ship MARSELLAISE. The ships company could see quite clearly the sunken blockships at the entrance to the canal, and the harbour was full of small craft that had been commandeered by the army and marines (it seemed as if everyone had their own private boat!). There was still the occasional pop of small arms fire from ashore, and at least one casualty was brought back to the ship while she was in the harbour. The opportunity was also taken to transfer some French casualties to their hospital ship.

The following day the remaining troops, primarily the ground crew for JEHU, were off loaded, thus completing the ship's allocated task. The whole operation was not without it's lighter side. Few who were onboard at the time will every forget the excited tones of the Gunnery Officer - "Stand To, Stand To. Aircraft Warning Red, Starboard Side. I think they're MiGs." Only to hear, a few minutes later, "Relax, it's only a flock of geese".

From November 8th to the end of the month OCEAN ferried men and transport from Port Said to Malta and Cyprus. During this period another milestone occurred, when two Army Austers landed on the ship off Famagusta. They were not aboard very long, but it marked the last landing and take off of a fixed wing aircraft from the ship. She finally sailed for the UK on December 1st with 600 men of 42 Commando, 200 Artillery troops and 5 Sycamore aircraft from JEHU.

By this time it had become clear that the United States was not backing the British and French Governments and the invasion came to a halt, with all troops withdrawn. When Nasser seized the Canal,

Anthony Eden firmly believed that Britain's interests were at stake. He feared that a hostile power in charge of Suez would seriously damage British trade during peace and her naval power during times of war. It was a humiliating climbdown for both the British and French governments.

H.M.S OCEAN returned to Devonport on December 7th to be welcomed by the Commander in Chief, Plymouth, Admiral Sir Mark Pizey, accompanied by the Commandant General Royal marines, Lieutenant General C. E. Hardy and the Flag Officer Helicopter Group Rear Admiral Sayer. Relatives and friends lined the Hoe and vantage points along the Hamoaze to wave as she proceeded upstream.

After a series of short speeches the troops were disembarked and the members of 42 Commando returned to their camp at Bickleigh - minus one green beret which had in it the badges of the Royal Marines and the Royal Tank Regiment . This they left on top of the 70 foot high statue of Ferdinand de Lesseps, the canal's engineer, at the head of the Suez Canal, to the frustration of the Egyptians who eventually demolished the statue with explosives.

En route for Cyprus. August 1956.

Loading lorry off Cyprus

Training Squadron, Portland. Stokers march past Captain E.G. Roper at Divisions. 1955

Crown Copyright

HMS Ocean at Portland only one aircraft on the Flight Deck. 1955.

Captain's Barge on deck.

HMS Ocean at Port Said. November 1956. Crown Copyright.

Operation Musketeer. Suez November 1956.

In company with HMS Theseus. Ocean leading.

Shipping sunk in Suez Canal. November 1956.

An oil painting depicting the landing of No 45 Royal Marine Commandos at Suez. November 1956. Copyright Trustees RM Funds.

HMS Ocean returns to Devonport after operation Musketeer. December 1956. Crown Copyright.

Royal Inspection and Final Curtain.

After leave and replenishment H.M.S OCEAN was back on duty in her training role by the middle of January 1957, and on February 1st embarked for Scotland and points north. After anchoring off North Berwick the ship proceeded to Antwerp and was open to visitors; and on March 23rd got under way for Plymouth. However as she passed down the Scheldt for the open sea the ship passed over an object presumed to be an uncharted wreck. Commander Carpenter remembered the incident well: "Clearing the harbour we travelled down the winding river through some low lying countryside. The pilot took one bend too wide and standing on the port side of the flight deck, admiring the view, I was amazed to see that we had ridden up on to the side of the bank. Looking down from one of the sponsons I could see a man riding his bike beneath me - he looked equally amazed. We slid up the bank with a slight list and much churning of muddy water from the propeller and then back into the channel. No damage seemed to have been done. That night, after having cleared the estuary, making our way back towards Plymouth, I had the Middle Watch in the engine room and at about 2 am was startled by a tremendous scraping noise along the bottom of the hull. The Shipwright Officer was sent for to check the watertight compartment where the plates had been pushed in and, with his staff, he rigged up a cement box to seal the leak. On arrival at Plymouth the hull was examined and several huge scratches were found along the bottom, which indicated that the mast of a wreck had done the damage. There was a board of enquiry but no blame was attached to the ship".

While the ship was in dock in Plymouth work was carried out to prepare the main hangar for what was to prove the final event in OCEAN's life. Her Majesty the Queen was to dine aboard with her Captains, and the main hangar was temporarily refitted to provide the venue. Wooden frames were erected along both sides, and covered with fabric to provide false bulkheads. Sufficient space was left behind them for waiters to rush around unseen.

On May 6th the ship left dry dock and on May 13th departed Devonport for Cromarty Firth to join exercises with the Home Fleet and to proceed to sea on the 24th for the rendezvous with the Royal Yacht Britannia. On the morning of the 27th the Fleet formed single line ahead and H.M.S OCEAN fired a 21 gun Royal salute to welcome Her Majesty the Queen and the Duke of Edinburgh on board the Royal Yacht. On the same evening, moored at Invergordon, the Royal Party were welcomed on board by OCEAN's Commanding Officer Captain Beloe, who escorted Her Majesty to B Hangar which had become a banqueting hall for the occasion. In addition to the fabric decorated walls, the after lift well was flooded and a footbridge erected over it - rumour had it that swans were placed on this artificial lake. Most of the ship's company did not actually see the Queen at Invergordon and only caught a glimpse on newsreels at a local cinema.

On the 28th at 15.00 Her Majesty returned to the ship with Prince Philip to inspect Divisions, and later in the evening all ships were illuminated in her honour. On the 29th , the final day of the Royal visit, the ship was dressed to cheer the Royal Yacht as she passed by.

On June 1st Captain Beloe relinquished his command to Captain Smallwood, and a week later the ship embarked for visits to Reykjavik, Trondheim and Hamburg before returning to Plymouth on July 22nd. In early September OCEAN slipped for Helsinki and on the way there seemed to be many sightings of Russian ships and aircraft. The 'cod' war was being carried out by the fishing fleets at the time and the Russian presence was also visible on the ship's visit to Reykjavik.

On September 24th a Royal guard from HMS VICTORY joined the ship for passage to Oslo for the funeral of King Haakon of Norway. The Flag Officer Commanding Reserve Fleet, Vice Admiral Onslow, and Admiral of the Fleet Lord Fraser of North Cape were also aboard, as were 20 officers and other ranks of the Green Howards. The funeral took place at 13.00 on October 1st. A minutes silence was observed for the late King followed by a 21 gun funeral salute, a National salute and a 21 gun Royal salute to King Olav the Fifth. The following day OCEAN left for Portsmouth in very heavy weather to disembark the Royal guard and the officers and men of the Green Howards.

The shipped slipped for Gibraltar on October 6th calling at Bilbao on her return journey and then in early November embarked for Rosyth, Liverpool and Portsmouth before her final journey home to Plymouth.

On that final journey the ship sailed into Plymouth sound and up the Hamoaze to secure alongside no 8 wharf on December 5th. When the ship paid off in Devonport it had a very long paying off pennant with a hydrogen balloon on the end. As the ship acknowledged the Commander in Chief, Plymouth, at Mount Wise the pendant was caught by an eddy and was stuck straight up in the air - a salute or a defiant gesture?

In early January 1958 the ship was accepted for extended reserve and in March put up for disposal. In the 'Marine News' of March 1960 it was reported that H.M.S OCEAN had been sold to Mr H. Pratt of Lambert and Bendall Ltd, ship brokers. It was understood that the intention was to convert the carrier to a fish factory and trawler mother ship. Scant details were available, but it seemed that she was to have been fitted out with equipment to deep freeze the catches of the attendant trawler, which would be brought to the mother ship either by helicopter or the trawlers themselves. The mother ship was intended to be ready for service in Spring 1961; would have a complement of 425 and would stay at sea for between 65 and 70 days. This plan never came to fruition. The deal fell through and after a short spell in Devonport dockyard H.M.S OCEAN was moved to Inverkeithing and then to Faslane on May 6th 1962 where between May and August she was finally broken up.

The ship had twelve years of varied and admirable service in the British Royal Navy. From her last combined action with H.M.S THESEUS at Suez in November 1956 emerged a new and exciting concept for British naval air power - the helicopter carrier.

Royal Review of the Home Fleet. 1957

HM Yacht Britannia and the Home Fleet. 1957. Crown Copyright.

Carriers in formation steam past the Royal Yacht. Crown Copyright.

Review by Her Majesty and prince Philip by jeep on the Flight Deck. 1957. Lt (E) A.S. Carpenter reporting the SSM(E) Division.

Her Majesty inspects the Ship's Company Divisions on the Flight Deck. 1957

HM The Queen about to board HMS Ocean. Crown Copyright

Crown Copyright.

Her Majesty and Prince Philip arrive on board HMS Ocean to dine with Officers from the assembled Fleet.

Crown Copyright.

Rough sea. Returning from King Haakon's Funeral in Norway. 1957.

Class 240 drill on the Flight Deck. July 1957.

Belgian Royal Navy Trainees practice in Whaler. Trondheim July 1957.

Breaking up. Faslane. July 1962.

HMS OCEAN 1945-57.

Facts and Figures.

Displacement	13190 tons. 17720 tons full load
Length	694.5 feet
Beam	80.5 feet.
Draught	23.5 Feet.
Engines	Parsons geared turbine, 2 shafts. Shaft horsepower 40000=25 knots.
Boilers	4 Admiralty 3 drum type. 400 1b working presuure. 700 degrees max superheat
Weapons	6x4 2pdr AA. 3x 12 pdr AA. 10x40mm/Bofors. 2x40mm/MK9

BuildersAlexander Stephen and Sons Ltd, Linthouse, Govan

August 7th 1942. Ordered.

November 8th 1942 Laid Down.

July 8th 1944. Launched.

Jun 30th 1945 Commissioned.

December 5th 1957 Paid off in Devonport.

January 1958 Accepted for Extended Reserve.

March 1958 Put up for Disposal.

May 1962Towed to Faslane by British Iron and Steel Corporation for scrapping. Completed by August 1962.

Pennant number R68.

Flight Deck code. ' 0'

Badge description. Field Blue.

Badge Issuant from water barry wavy in true white and blue, a representative of Neptune white.

Motto. The badge is in allusion to the name, showing as it does Neptune King of the Ocean.

Battle Honours Ushant 1781
Suez Canal 1915
Mesopotamia 1914
Dardanelles 1915
Korea 1952-53

HMS Ocean 1998

The Phoenix Arises

The sixth ship to carry the name OCEAN is the Royal Navy's new Helicopter Carrier, officially termed a Landing Platform Helicopter (LPH). It is the largest Royal Naval ship to be built since HMS HERMES in 1957, and is the first purpose built amphibious helicopter carrier designed for rapid landing of assault force by land or sea. She is scheduled to enter Service in 1999.

It was originally conceived in the mid eighties as a replacement for HMS HERMES which was sold to India in 1986. The ship was constructed on the Clyde at Kvaerner Govan, the Norwegian shipping, ship building and engineering conglomerate. Built in eight prefabricated sections, the first, the keel section was laid early in 1995. It was launched in a low key ceremony on October 11th 1995 without the usual Naming ceremony; and a slight accident occurred during launch, resulting in damage confined to a buckle of plates near the keel. In November 1996 the ship sailed from Govan, under it's own power, for VSEL's Buccleuch dock at Barrow in Furness to complete outfitting, installation of combat systems and communications and aviation requirement.

The primary role of the ship is to have the flexibility and speed for an Embarked Military Force (EMF) of 480 (800 in an emergency) personnel with 12 medium support helicopters(Sea Kings/Merlin MK4's) and 6 (Lynx/Gazelle/Apache) helicopters of the UK/NL Amphibious Force to conduct an amphibious assault. The ship could also be used to ferry Sea Harriers and Chinook helicopters, and provide a base for anti-terrorist operations.

In a non military Crisis the ship has the capacity to carry a high number of vehicles and personnel to an emergency zone; and to use it's helicopters for rescue purposes deep into a country's terrain. The ship's medical teams and logistic supplies would be crucial in such a civilian catastrophe.

HMS OCEAN has been designed to accommodate Royal Marines, and all of their equipment. There is a large stairwell leading directly into the forward end of the hangar, double width; and hatchway deckheads, enlarged to allow for fully laden marines, each carrying 120 pounds of ammunition and equipment for easy access to their assembly points. Four MKV Landing Craft Vehicle Personnel (LCVP), built by Vosper Thorneycraft, will be housed in recesses aft with davits and winch. The vehicle deck is loaded through a quarter ramp with access to flight deck and there is an internal ramp to flight deck with loading points for stores to be air lifted ashore. The huge hangar, the most extensive in naval service since the old ARK ROYAL, is capable of accommodating 12 support helicopters and the flight deck has 6 operating spots for the support helicopters and anti tank light helicopters of the UK/NL Amphibious force. There is also a large stern ramp to allow unloading into waiting landing craft or onto a floating pontoon.

On February 20th 1998 the VSEL yard was privileged to welcome Her Majesty Queen Elizabeth and His Royal Highness the Duke of Edinburgh to Barrow for the Naming ceremony. On that day the ship was named H.M.S OCEAN; christened by a bottle of Moet and Chandon champagne released by the ship's telegraph over the bow of the ship. During her visit Her Majesty was taken on a conducted tour of the ship by her first Commanding officer Captain Robert Turner, R.N., whose previous sea going appointment had been H.M.S ENDURANCE .

After her departure from the Barrow yard, H.M.S OCEAN will be based at Devonport Plymouth, home of the Navy's Commodore Amphibious Task Group (COMATG) as part of the UK's plan to develop a National Amphibious Ready group for the 21st century. Flying trials and Part IV trials will continue until February 1999, including Embarked Force trials in both Arctic and tropical conditions, and in mid 1999 the ship will head a major amphibious exercise in the Mediterranean that is planned to include an amphibious assault in Egypt as part of a growing training package with Egyptian forces.

OCEAN will become the linchpin of the Amphibious Squadron, its function to poise off a coast for considerable periods - moving swiftly into a dangerous area. It will be self sustained, without the need of ports or airfields as bases, and will be able to employ her full weight with strikes ashore.

VSEL's original statement on build was "to provide an overview of the approach to meeting the Ministry of Defence's requirement. The objective was to deliver on time to the Royal Navy, an innovative, reliable, affordable and compliant amphibious helicopter carrier; fit for purpose, designed and built to ensure the highest quality and safety standards"

The core of the ships operation is the combat system comprising the personnel, equipment, weapons and sensors which enable HMS OCEAN to conduct a two company beach assault whilst defending herself against a variety of threats. The amphibious assault in which the EMF of 800 Royal Marines and other units are landed is achieved using support helicopters and landing craft from HMS OCEAN. The battle-cube is monitored using ships sensors and data received from other ships. Data from these sources is processed and distributed using the Command Support System(CSS) allowing the command to direct the ships effort and weapons systems

Whenever at sea the Operations Complex will be the focal point for all operational tasks, especially the management of the airspace and control of aircraft allocated to H.M.S OCEAN. This comprises three primary tactical areas namely the Operations Room, the Amphibious Operations Room and the Main Communications Office.

Within the Operations Room the command system displays the electronically processed picture from Radar 996. This is integrated with the data link picture received remotely from other ships, either on national or NATO communications networks, and the position of any other radar transmitters detected by the passive electronic surveillance suite. All the information is processed by high speed Ferranti computers, enhanced with graphical symbology and displayed to the operators on colour screens. The aim is to produce a clear and accurate computer picture to the Command to facilitate the tactical direction of the ship and its assets.

Those in the Main Communications Office (MCO) are responsible for maintaining 24 hour strategic communication links with the UK and NATO by satellite and high frequency means. Signal messages are distributed electronically by the DIMPS processing system. The MCO is also at the heart of the shorter range high and ultra high frequency radio links with other ship and aircraft in company providing circuits for use by operators throughout the ship.

The ship is conned and navigated from the Bridge which is equipped with its own radar displays and automated plotting table which can be fed from the Global Positioning System(GPS)

The Warfare Support Department has a unique whole-ship role which co-ordinates all departmental activities together into a cohesive operational unit as well as providing specialist skills in areas such as seamanship, medical, regulating, chaplaincy and physical training disciplines.

9 Assault Squadron Royal Marines (9ASRM) is the integral Royal Marine Squadron permanently embarked in HMS OCEAN. In addition to whole-ship responsibilities including fire-fighting, bridge watchkeeping and security, 9ASRM provide four MK5 LCVP for the ship to shore movement of embarked forces. It also provides essential amphibious knowledge and experience with which to advice the Command. The Squadron is also capable of a number of secondary tasks such as boarding parties, using the LCVPs to support a Commando Unit ashore, and conducting beach reconnaissance. 9ASRM is divided into a Headquarters Unit, a Landing Craft Troop, Vehicle Deck Party and Assault Supply Team.

The LCVP MK5 is a significant improvement on it's predecessor, utilising a water jet propulsion system to produce a craft capable of achieving in excess of 25 knots. The craft can carry up to 35 fully equipped troops distances up to 200 nautical miles and with their modern navigation equipment including radar, GPS and planed future fit computer charts, over the horizon operations are a real possibility. Alternatively the craft can carry vehicles such as landrovers with trailers, 105rm light guns or trucks carrying up to 8.2 tonnes of stores. H.M.S OCEAN has a dedicated vehicle deck which can accommodate Embarked Forces vehicles up to 40 land rover variants, 34 trailers and six 105m light guns.

As a purpose built Helicopter Carrier H.M.S OCEAN was designed from the outset to embark, support and operate both troop carrying and attack helicopters. Secondary roles include ferrying Sea Harriers, providing a base for an anti submarine helicopter squadron or to act as an aviation training ship. With 6 helicopter operating spots on the deck HMS OCEAN also has hangarage for 12 medium sized helicopters or 15 Sea Harriers. During the assault phase of an amphibious operation HMS OCEAN could launch two waves of troop carrying Sea Kings from 845/846 Squadrons as well as operating the smaller armed and reconnaissance Lynx and Gazelles of 847 Squadron. Access to the Flight Deck is by two aircraft lifts from the hangar.

An absence of traditional aircraft workshops coupled with the requirement for amphibious squadrons to embark much of their deployable support equipment and spares in other platforms has led to the development of a new concept for the engineering support of amphibious aviation at sea. A further new departure for the Royal Navy is the siting of Flyco at the back of an integrated bridge.

Although H.M.S OCEAN has no aircraft permanently allocated she would normally embark an Air Group from the Commando Helicopter Force. 845/846 Naval Air Squadrons each operate Sea King aircraft which can carry 16 fully equipped troops or an underslung load of 45001b. 847 operate Gazelles and the TOW missile armed Lynx 7. HMS OCEAN can also operate RAF CH47 Chinooks or Pumas and any helicopters of the Army Air Corps.

Whether it be operational logistics support to an Embarked Military Force, detailed planning for a sustained out-of-area deployment abroad or the full gamut of daily domestic services onboard the Supply Department will be at the forefront of all activities in HMS OCEAN. Beyond the traditional tasks of pay, cash, catering and naval stores the ship brings the additional challenge of rapidly fluctuating EMF numbers onboard, significant support required for the embarked Air Group and the spare capacity to move quickly to one of her secondary roles such as humanitarian aid.

The ship has a unique system of automated storing routes, the latest equipment in a centralised galley serving three adjacent dining halls, a full bakery and a dedicated Emergency Feeding Station. Other areas include the Naval Storerooms, Catering Provisions Complex, Wardroom, Bridge Mess, Aircrew Refreshment Bar and the NAAFI compartments. On the administrative front there is a separate Captain's Office and Unit Personnel/Cash Office.

A few facts and figures start to illustrate the supply task onboard with custody and issue of 17, 000 line items of stores, the 24 hour provision of up to 4, 000 hot meals a day, the control of 16 tons of operational ration packs and a significant amount of cash, both Sterling and Foreign Currency.

H.M.S OCEAN is propelled by two Crossley Pielstick medium speed diesels, each of 12 cylinders, and is capable of reaching a speed of 18 knots. Each engine has a maximum continuous rating of 6750 KW and drives through a 3.1 reduction gearbox via a solid propeller shaft to a 5 bladed skewed fixed pitch propeller. It should be noted that there is no reversing capability in the gearbox; it is the engine that needs to rotate in the opposite direction to generate astern thrust. There are 4 Rushton generators, each capable of producing 2MW, which provide to turn radars, operate aircraft lifts, operate the Galley and support ventilation heating and domestic facilities.

The main engines and diesel generators are controlled from the Ships Control Centre and are overseen by the Machinery Control and Surveillance System and there is a closed circuit TV monitoring system covering all the main auxiliary machinery spaces.

As well as the Propulsion Section the other major equipment is Assault Systems which deals with all plant and systems outside the propulsion section including the Landing Craft, ramps and aircraft lifts. Each aircraft lift weighs 50 tonnes and has a maximum load of 19 tonnes. They are supported on cantilevers driven by large bicycle type chains and powered by a single hydraulic pump. They take approximately one minute to travel from the hangar to the flight deck.

Unusually for a warship H.M.S OCEAN has two large Brown Brothers stabilizers, which are fully retractable when going astern or berthing, and a Stone Vickers bow thruster. The ship can carry 1500 tonnes of aviation fuel and an equal amount of diesel fuel resulting in a range of 8, 000 mile at a cruising speed of 15 knots.

The Weapons Engineering Department is responsible for the operational availability and maintenance of the ship's combat system, comprising sensors, weapons and communications systems. The entire spectrum of engineering disciplines from the mechanical and hydraulic components of guns and weapons lifts, through microwave and signal processing techniques, satellite communications links down to the microprocessor logic circuits and computer software programmes are covered onboard. By necessity there are considerable in-built self testing facilities and automatic fault diagnosis systems throughout the equipment. The multitude of aerials fitted to the superstructure reveal the very latest in radar and communications equipment. Less visible is the extensive range of sophisticated electronic equipment fitted throughout H.M.S OCEAN each forming a vital constituent part of the ship's Combat System. There are medium range and navigational radars onboard each having dedicated autoextractors for automatic tracking of targets. H.M.S OCEAN is the first warship to be fitted with Spree Laser Gyro Compasses which provide the ships heading attitude and reference data. A fully computerised Command System links all of the weapons and sensors, presenting the Command with a clear air, surface and sub-surface picture which enables the ship to function in a multi threat environment.

As a footnote, the large ship's bell from HMS OCEAN 1945 was handed over to her successor at the Fleet Air Arm Museum, Yeovilton. The bell was bought by Lieutenant Commander Peter London when the ship paid off for the list time, and lodge at the museum on condition that it was to be passed to the new ship at a future date. The bell was accepted by the Commanding Officer of the new HMS OCEAN, Captain R.M. Turner, in 1998.

The small bell from HMS OCEAN 1945 was presented to Fitzwilliam College, Cambridge, in 1961 by Caspar John who was at that time First Sea Lord, in appreciation of the great deal of help that the ship had received from the University who had accepted Electrical officers as undergraduates. It hangs outside the dining hall entrance.

LPH.309. Kaervenor. Govan Yard. 1995
Crown Copyright

LPH 309 at Kaervenor-Govan Yard. Spring 1995.

Main Gangway. July 1996.

Engine Room. July 1996.

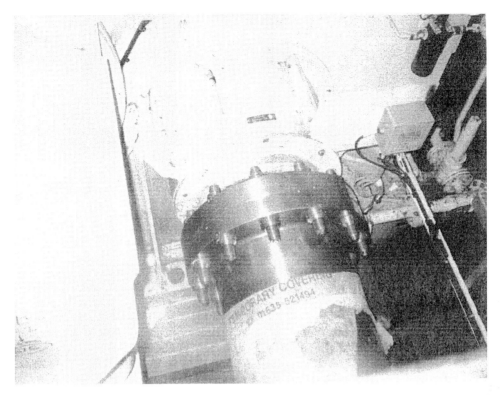

Engine Room. Shaft. July 1996.

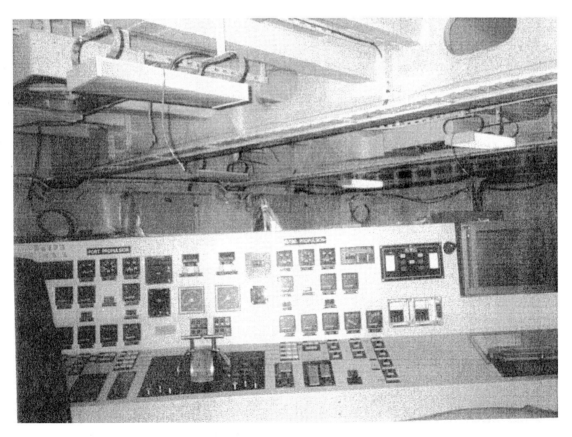

Main Engine room control. July 1996.

Port propeller shaft. July 1996.

Main Hanger. July 1996.

Propeller shaft. July 1996.

LPH 309. Launch. Kaervenor. Govan Yard October 1995
Crown Copyright.

LPH 309. Launch. Kaervenor. Govan Yard October 1995
Crown Copyright.

En route from Govan to VSEL Barrow. November 1996. Crown Copyright.

Arrival at VSEL Barrow for fitting out. November 1996. Crown Copyright.

The Hanger lift. VSEL Barrow in Furness.
Copyright VSEL.

Visit by HRH Duke of Edinburgh. November 1997. Copyright VSEL.

The Naming Ceremony. 2oth February 1998.
Crown Copyright.

Facts and Figures 1998

Displacement.21, 578 tonnes.
Length208m
Beam34.4m
Draught6.6m
Complement284

Weapons.

Three 20mm Vulvan Phalanx close in weapon system
Twin barrel 30mu BMARC guns
Passive Decoys.

Sensors

Radar 996 (Combined Air/Surface
Radar 1007 (Navigation and Helicopter control)
UAT Electronic Support Measures

Command and Control

4 ENA Multi Function Command System
SHF/UHF/VHF/MF Communications systems
Data Links
GMDSS Phase II
Command Support System

Aircraft and Landing Craft

12 Sea King HC4 medium Support Helicopters
6 Lynx AH7 or 6 Gazelle Light Helicopters
or
12 Sea Harriers (Ferry Role)
4 Mark V Landing Craft Vehicle Personnel

Affiliations

City of Sunderland
The Worshipful Company of Farriers.
Coldstream Guards
Pangbourne College
30 Squadron Royal Air Force
Brymon Airways
H.M.S. Ocean Association

Appendix A

List of Captains and Executive Officers in command from 1945 to 1957

October 1944 Commander N. S. Henderson
May 1945 Captain Casper John
15th November 1946 Captain A. W. Clarke O.B.E. D.S.O.
April 1948 Captain W. R. C. Leggatt D.S.O.
1st July 1948 Commander G. V. Parmiter*
21st November 1949 Captain R. F. Elkins O.B.E
3rd April 1950 Captain B. E. W. Logan
1st August 1950 Captain R. C. V. Ross D.S.O.
22 December 1950 Commander J.O.C. Hayes, O.B.E., R.N.**
18th June 1951 Captain C. L. G. Evans D.S.O. D.S.C.
3rd December 1952 Captain B. E. W. Logan
9th January 1954 Commander G. Kilmartin***
1st May 1954 Captain H. C. Browne C.B.E. D.S.O.
4th April 1955 Captain R. G. Roper D.S.O. D.S.C.
8th October 1956 Captain I. W. T. Beloe D.S.C.
1st June 1957 Captain J. Smallwood

* Commander Parmiter is described ' In Command' in the October 1949 *Navy List* and is presumably filing in until Captain Elkins arrival.

** Commander Hayes is shown as ' In Command' in the April 1951 *Navy List*. He was the ship's Executive Officer from December 1950 until March 1952.

*** Command Kilmartin is shown as ' In Command in the April 1954 *Navy List*. He had left the ship by the following (July) edition.

HMS Ocean replenishment in Korean waters. 1953. Crown Copyright.

Appendix B

Squadrons embarked in H.M.S. Ocean 1945-1956

1792 SquadronNightfighters.
Fairey Firefly F's
11th December 1945 until April 1946.
Disbanded UK 17th April 1946
Commanding Officer: Lieutenant Commander S. Dixon-Child, RN

1702 Squadron Sea Otter (dt3)
25th July 1946 until 12th September 1946
Disbanded 12th September 1946
Commanding Officer: Lieutenant (A) R.S. Kilburn, R.N.V.R

892 SquadronNightfighters
Hellcat 11's
22nd November 1945 to 16th April 1946
Disbanded Donibristle 19th April 1946
Commanding Officer: Major J.O. Armour, R.M. (one of several distinguished and successful R.M. officers serving as pilots in the Fleet Air Arm).

805 Squadron 20th Carrier Air Group
Seafire FXV. Firefly FR1 and Firefly NF1
19th June 1946 to 28th June 1948
Disbanded Eglington 1st July 1948
Commanding Officers: Lieutenant Commander (A) P.J. Hutton, D.S.C., R.N.V.R (until 28th September 1947) then Lieutenant Commander P.E.I. Bailey, RN
The squadron was temporarily disembarked in April 1946 when Seafires were banned from deck landings due to technical problems. Firefly FR1s and NF1's were used until the arrival of Seafire F17's in April 1947. This Squadron patrolled the roads leading to Haifa, protecting the withdrawal of troops during the last days of the Palestine Mandate in May 1948.

816 Squadron20th Carrier Air Group
Firefly FR1's and Firefly NF1's
19th June 1946 to 28th June 1948.
Disbanded at Lee-on-Solent 28th June 1948
Commanding Officers: Lieutenant Commander J.S.L. Crabbe, RN (until 6th January 1947) then
Lieutenant Commander (A) S. Hook, RN
In November 1946 four Firefly NF1's were transferred to 805 Squadron but were returned to 816 Squadron in May 1947.

812 Squadron 14th Carrier Air Group Black Flight
Four Firefly NF1's
(DLP) 19th August 1948
(DT) 3rd to 6th January 1949 to H.M.S. TRIUMPH
10th April 1949 returned to H.M.S. OCEAN
Commanding Officers: Lieutenant Commander F.B.G. Sheffield, D.S.C., RN (until 6th March 1949) then
Lieutenant Commander R.M. Fell, RN

804 Squadron 14th Carrier Air Group
Seafire FR47's and Seafury FB11's
24th August 1948 until 3rd January 1949
3rd to 6th January 1949 H.M.S. TRIUMPH
10th April 1949 return to H.M.S. OCEAN
20th December 1949 to H.M.S. GLORY
Commanding Officers: Lieutenant Commander S.F.F. Shotton, RN (until 6th February 1949) then
Lieutenant Commander C.F. Hargreaves, RN

898 Squadron 17th Carrier Air Group
Sea Fury FB11's
24th July 1951 to 26th February 1952
26th February 1952 to H.M.S. THESEUS
6th July 1952 H.M.S. GLORY
9th December 1952 returned to HM.S. OCEAN
Disbanded 1st January 1953
Commanding Officer: Lieutenant Commander T.L.M. Brander, D.S.C., RN

807 Squadron17th Carrier Air Group
Sea Fury F.B.11's
24th July 1951 to 24th February 1952
24th February 1952 to H.M.S. THESEUS
6th July 1952 to H.M.S. GLORY
9th December 1952 to H.M.S. OCEAN
24th to 30th July 1953 detached to K6
Commanding Officers: Lieutenant Commander A.J. Thompson (until 1st January 1953) then
Lieutenant Commander T.L.M. Brander, D.S.C, RN

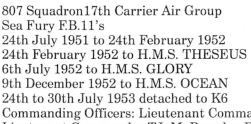

810 Squadron17th Carrier Air Group
Firefly AS5's and Firefly FR5's
25th July 1951 to 6th July 1952
6th July 1952 to H.M.S. GLORY
15th October 1952 to H.M.S. THESEUS
9th December 1952 to H.M.S. OCEAN
24th to 30th July 1953 detached to KT (DT)
29th August 1953 detached toK6 and K16
9th September 1953 to H.M.S. OCEAN
Disbanded in UK 17th December 1953
Commander Officers: Lieutenant Commander D. E. Johnson, RN (until 18th June 1952) then
Lieutenant Commander A.W. (Pants) Bloomer

802 Squadron
Sea Fury FB11's
4th April 1952 to 1st December 1952
1st December 1952 to H.M.S. THESEUS
Squadron disbanded UK 10th December 1952.
Commanding Officers: Lieutenant Commander S.F.F. Shotton, D.S.C., RN (until 22nd July 1952) then
Lieutenant Commander D.A. Dick, D.S.C, RN, (killed 24th July 1952) then
Lieutenant Commander P.H. London, D.S.C, RN
The squadron was a joint recipient of the 1952 Boyd Trophy

825 Squadron
Firefly AS5's and FR5's
18th February 1952 to 1st December 1952
1st December 1952 to H.M.S. THESEUS
Disbanded in UK 10th December 1952
Commanding Officer: Lieutenant Commander K. Roberts, RN
The squadron was a joint recipient of the 1952 Boyd Trophy

845 Squadron
Whirlwind HAS22 and HAR 3
19th June 1956 to 5th July 1956 (split between H.M.S. OCEAN and H.M.S THESEUS)
5th July 1956 to Lee-on-Solent
29th September 1956 re-embarked
18th October 1956 to H.M.S. THESEUS for work up and training with the Royal Marine Commandos.
Commanding Officer: Lieutenant Commander J.C. Jacob, RN
Four helicopters were embarked for a visit to Hamburg in June 1956, then again briefly before transferring to the Mediterranean in H.M.S. THESEUS for work up and training with the Royal Marine
Commandos.

JEHUJoint Experimental Helicopter Unit (later the ' Experimental' was dropped).
Westland Sycamore HR14s and Whirlwind HAR2's.
A mixed group drawing personnel from the Army and R.A.F., set up at Nether Wallop, Hampshire.
These helicopters, together with Whirlwinds from 845, ferried Royal Marines ashore during the Suez
Crises in the first ever helicopter borne assault from the sea.

Appendix C

Honours in Korea for members of the Ship's company

Captain Charles Leo Gandore Evans D.S.O. D.S.C. C.B.E.
Captain Brian Ewen Welson Evans Mention in Dispatches.
Lieutenant Commander (P) Cedric Kenelm Roberts D.S.O.
Lieutenant Commander (P) Andrew William Bloomer D.S.C.
Lieutenant Commander Richard Arnold Lea M.B.E.
Lieutenant Commander (E) (A/E) Philip Leslie Luby M.B.E.
Lieutenant Commander (P) Donald Arthur Dick D.S.C. Mention in Dispatches.
Lieutenant Commander (E) Ronald Albert Harcus Mention in Dispatches.
Lieutenant (P) Peter Carmichael D.S.C.
Lieutenant (P) Peter Steel Davis D.S.C.
Lieutenant (P) Richard Rowan Hawkesworth D.S.C.
Lieutenant (P) Michael Lawrence Brown Mention in Dispatches.
Lieutenant (P) Robert Henry Hallam Mention in Dispatches.
Lieutenant (P) David Thomas McKeown Mention in Dispatches.
Lieutenant (P) Norman Edmund Peniston-Bird. Mention in Dispatches.
Lieutenant (P) John Lewis Treloar Mention in Dispatches.
Lieutenant (P) Peter Watkinson Mention in Dispatches.
Lieutenant (O) William James Cooper Mention in Dispatches.
Master At Arms. Ivor George Howells Mention in Dispatches.
Aircrewman (1) Charles Patrick McCullagh D.S.M.
Aircrewman (1) James Patrick Potter D.S.M.
Chief Yeoman of Signals Jack Stephens D.S.M. B.E.M.
Chief Air Fitter (E) Ronald Brighton B.E.M.
Chief Engine Room Artificer James Pooley Rowe Mention in Dispatches.
Chief Aircraft Artificer Ian Ivor Basil Pearce Hamon Mention in Dispatches.
Chief Aircraft Artificer Frank Webb Mention in Dispatches.
Chief Aircraft Artificer David William Wynne Mention in Dispatches.
Chief Engine Room Artificer Douglas Perrin B.E.M. Mention in Dispatches.
Aircraft Mechanician (1) Thomas Lewin Sampson Mention in Dispatches.
Radio Electrical (Air) (3) John Edwin Lucken Mention in Dispatches.
Chief Airfitter (O) Stanley Reid Mention in Dispatches.
Chief Petty Officer Airman Alan Dixon Mention in Dispatches.
Supply Chief Petty Officer Henry Roy Ronald Williams Mention in Dispatches.
Leading Airman (O) Reginald Arthur Fountain Mention in Dispatches.

Bibliography

Battleships and Battle Cruisers of the Royal Navy since 1861 by Commander. B.R. Coward, RN
Face the Music. A Sailor's Story by Vice Admiral Sir John Hayes, RN
Caspar John by Rebecca John
A Sailor's Survival by Captain R.N. Catlow, RN
With the Carriers in Korea 1950 - 53 by J.R.P. Lansdown
The Fleet Air Arm Since 1945 by Paul Beaver
Vampire LZ551/G by Squadron Leader M.J. Briggs
Royal Navy Aircraft Since 1945 by Ray Williams
Ocean Saga January 1953
Ocean Saga May 1951 - October 1953
Stand Easy 1955
Ocean News Annual 1956
The National Service Sailor by P.M. Cobbold
The Squadrons of the Fleet Air Arm by Ray Sturtivant and Theo Ballance.

Dressed Overall. Grand Harbour. Valletta.

Acknowledgements

My thanks to Rear Admiral Euan Maclean, CB, RN, for his help and ecnouragement and for kindly writing the foreword to this book.

I must also thank all the members of the HMS OCEAN Association who recorded their memories for me by letter and cassette and for the flood of photographs, many of which make up the record of this book. My especial thanks to Shipmates Tony Smyth, BEM and Malcolm Clarke for their invaluable help in putting the book together.

I am also indebted to the Ministry of Defence, the Greenwich Maritime Museum and VSEL Barrow for permission to reproduce copyright photographs, and Lieutenant Colonel A.J.F. Noyes, RM for permission to reproduce the photograph of the original painting of the Suez Landing which hangs in the Condor Officers Mess, 45 Commando, Royal Marines, at Arbroath.

HMS Ocean lying at her moorings in Venice May 1949.